BOYS WILL BE MEN
A Son Comes of Age in His Own Words

Compiled and Edited by
Marjorie Lynn

Marjorie A. Lynn

ISBN: 1-4107-3254-1 (e-book)
ISBN: 1-4107-3255-X (Paperback)

Library of Congress Control Number: 2003091773

This book is printed on acid free paper.

Printed in the United States of America
Bloomington, IN

1stBooks – rev. 05/22/03

For Bruce, without whom this book would not be.
And for Ed, without whom Bruce would not be —
and for Lori, Isley and Chase; Sharyl, Scott, Katrina and Max.

Contents

Acknowledgments

I want to express my gratitude to my son, Bruce, for allowing me to share his letters from Africa. He gave us insight into who we are as a family and what was important to him as he grew up.

Several special friends and colleagues offered me their energy and evaluation as the book progressed. My thanks go to Helen French, Arlene Santa Fe, Irene Troy, Annie Middleton, and Judy Hallberg for sharing their thoughts with me after reading parts of the book, and to Valerie Lankford for nurturing my efforts. Vivian Wheeler offered invaluable ideas and editorial assistance, for which I am also very grateful.

I turned to my husband and Bruce's father, Ed, and to daughter Sharyl for advice and counsel as I sorted through the letters to edit out those parts that would be of limited interest to the reader. I am extremely grateful to them for their support and encouragement. I am also indebted to Bruce's wife, Lori, who was a valued sounding board, and to Sharyl's husband, Scott, who helped design the cover and layout of the book.

My heartfelt thanks go to all family members, immediate and extended, for their contributions to our family's values. I hope I have achieved my purpose in publishing Bruce's letters, which is to show how everyone with whom children make a connection can have a significant impact on their character development and attainment of adulthood, ready to start a family of their own.

African American and Latino and Asian American children should know about European history and cultures, and white children should know about the histories and cultures of diverse peoples of color with whom they must share a city, a nation, and a world.

—*Marian Wright Edelman,* The Measure of Our Success

Introduction

Hidden behind some shoes and an old computer in a closet I am finally cleaning out, I find an unmarked box, which I pull out and open. I discover letters from our son, Bruce, written more than two decades ago from Africa when he was 20 years old. Already sitting on the floor to sort shoes, I stall the task at hand and begin reading. It is hours before I finish. And weeks of thinking about the letters, and our son's adventure.

I soon recognized that the letters would represent a journey of discovery for others traveling toward themselves, and would be of interest to parents and friends of young men and women who are in the throes of their own coming of age. I, therefore, set about sorting through the letters with a view to sharing them with a wider audience.

When I came to compiling the letters, I consulted with Bruce in making minor changes needed for consistency and flow, for removal of redundancies, and for correction of occasional lapses in spelling and grammar. These changes have not in any way altered the basic sense or meaning of the letters.

Bruce's journey began with an exhaustive search for a destination in which to spend a year abroad between his sophomore and junior years at Harvard University. His first goal was to go somewhere that he could speak French to deepen his skills in that language, but also somewhere that was culturally very different from what he knew. While the French colonial heritage had brought the French language to virtually every continent, Bruce was most drawn to Africa; it seemed to him to have just the right balance of exotic and connected: exotic in the tales of jungle and indigenous tribal life, connected through the American heritage of African Americans.

As he investigated possibilities, his focus on Africa was confirmed when he learned that some of the most stable African countries in 1981 were francophone. Their stability was due largely to France's ongoing development and investment support in its former colonies, which included Senegal, Cameroon, Upper Volta (now Burkina Faso), Ivory Coast, Benin, and Togo.

These countries became the target of his quest for a year abroad. Every possible link, connection, and contact with these countries that he could find, he explored throughout the summer. This was the time before email, so he did everything by posted letter. He made over a hundred inquiries. Then a lead from a lead from a lead referred him to David Apter, whose ten-person public relations firm in Washington, D. C.—David Apter and Associates (DA&A)—had as its largest account the Republic of Togo.

Togo is a tiny country in West Africa with little natural wealth. It has a relatively healthy infrastructure because of its good port and some cash from a small but rich phosphate deposit. At that time it wanted to invest in becoming a tourist and business center for western Africa, but to do so it first needed to inform Americans about Togo, so it contacted DA&A to promote the country. One of the first things DA&A did was set up and run the Togo Information Service.

Bruce's connection gained him an interview with David's son, Marc, who explained that the firm was having great difficulty getting relevant, useful information out of Togo. Also, a common public relations (PR) tactic to promote tourism to a given location is to run a travel writers' trip there. When DA&A did that, all the government wanted to do was arrange trips to the president's birthplace and the new cement factory, places of obvious pride to the Togolese, but pretty boring to travel writers. Marc asked Bruce if he would be interested in going to Togo to live, to drum up interesting stories and pull together itineraries for travel writers' visits. In addition, the firm needed him to bridge the 7,000-mile, five-time-zone, telex-driven communication gap and to assist with various other account activities. It would involve his living at the University of Benin in the Village du Benin, just outside Lomé, the capital of Togo.

The interview went well, and Bruce was invited to Washington for a "chat" in French with the director of the Togo Information Service to make sure he could manage the language. He credits the success of that interview to his continuing French studies at college, but also to his high school French teachers and the school's tradition of having juniors gain full immersion in the language by living abroad for two weeks with a French family.

Within the week, David Apter called to offer Bruce the job in Togo. Before leaving the country, Bruce spent two months in Washington working with the people at DA&A and being briefed. He greatly admired Apter and felt privileged to be working for him. Now deceased, during his life David was a respected civil rights activist who used his PR expertise to support many causes.

Bruce's adventure was more than travel to an exotic locale for interesting work and study. The people he met and with whom he became friends were lifelong influences. He had found an ideal means to discover Africa. Getting there tested his patience more than it had ever been tested before, and he later told us that the experience of working so hard to acquire the position validated the truth of an African proverb that "patience is the key to paradise."

In the letters that follow, Bruce gives his family the gift of his thoughts, dreams, and challenges, as well as a preview of his destiny as a man. Part of our role as parents, I believe, is to do all we can to ensure that our children's destinies are not thwarted, interrupted, or halted, so that every child can grow up to become the person he or she is meant to be. The unfolding of that person is truly a wonder to behold.

Bruce's isolation in Africa triggered a rare outpouring of thoughts and sharing; every young person who is at the age of becoming is — usually silently, and always individualistically — pondering, evaluating, and dreaming, just as Bruce did. Every parent, as well as everyone who follows a young person's life with interest and affection, sees glimpses of this hidden blooming. Because the fast, efficient new technologies of communication were years away, Bruce had to rely on the time-honored writing of letters to communicate. What a blessing that was for us.

We learned from his letters who Bruce is and who he thinks we are. We saw our family values and experiences viewed through his eyes, along with his own memories, passions, and appreciation. In his own words, Bruce shares his transition from boyhood to manhood.

I
A Motivating Thirst

I was a young man in search of a soul, and I found my own. I grew up during those months in Europe—a maturation that made itself most plain during my days at Dachau...Every adolescent male ages 18-21 must find his Europe and his Dachau. If we are to help the next generation, we give them testing grounds for identity.

—*Michael Gurian* A Fine Young Man

Bruce grew up north of Boston in Ipswich, Massachusetts, on a rural road that was a long bus ride to school and town. His sister and only sibling, Sharyl, is four years younger. His father, Ed, and I in 1972 chose to live in Ipswich because it was the most heterogeneous small town in the area. More important, its school system had a good reputation. Bruce thrived in the friendly Ipswich environment, and in its schools.

Rounding out our household the year Bruce went abroad was our dog, Sparkle, a mixed breed that resembled a coyote when curled up asleep, and Anna, our elderly Siamese cat, who until the arrival of Nerissa thought she ruled the Lynn household. Nerissa was a fluffy Maine coon cat that Bruce and college roommate Steve Keeler shared. Since both Bruce and Steve took the same year abroad, Mom and Dad Lynn assumed guardianship of Nerissa.

Besides Bruce's immediate family and school friends, his circle of companions included buddies at the Northshore Unitarian Universalist Church, where his father has been the minister since we moved to Ipswich, as well as an extended family of friends.

At college, he was especially close to members of the Phoenix (PSK) Club. In their sophomore year, Bruce and Steve both pledged to this "finals club," a male bastion on campus similar to a fraternity house but without residences. His dad and I saw PSK as a major addition to college life for Bruce, giving him a place to develop friendships and the space to sprawl his 6' 4" frame in big, comfy chairs. We also noticed his new ease with social graces, which we at home had been less than successful in conveying. And it was a place to do his laundry.

Fred Chadwick and Don Wood were Ed's college roommates at Syracuse University School of Architecture, and they remain two of our family's dearest friends. To our children, these adopted "uncles" are a part of our family. Bruce learned early how deep relationships thrive, endure, and affect us. He reminisces about this influence in his first flurry of letters and paints a picture of how he formed his ideals of work and rest.

His participation in high school student government became his ideal of work. He loved participating in the Student Council and being involved in state and national student government activities and conventions. Whether at a student conference in Texas, or in an elected position on the Student Advisory Board that provided a student voice on the local school committee, Bruce honed his leadership skills and learned to listen to conflicting viewpoints in a political environment.

He also learned how to be proactive in solving problems. I remember one of the issues that came out of the Advisory Board meetings was the breakdown in communication between school, parents, and students. To open up the lines, Bruce initiated and then edited with classmate Karl Muench the first student-produced page in the local paper. The publisher of the *Ipswich Chronicle* at the time, Bill Wasserman, became a teacher and mentor, helping Bruce, often late into the evening, to publish the weekly student news page — "The Ramblin' Clam," named for Ipswich's famous clams.

Yet Bruce was a typical teenager, who often sat at the dinner table with absolutely nothing to say to his family. His lack of conversation was certainly an effective form of teenage rebellion in a communicative family. During most of his junior year and half of his senior year in high school, we were lucky to know anything about what he was thinking or feeling. We were pleased that this stage passed before he left for college.

His ideal of rest he found in Vermont. Fred's place on little Huff Pond in Sudbury afforded our children in the summer a swimming hole amidst the beauty of the Green Mountains. And during winter visits, a snow-crystal wonderland. When Bruce was around 12 and Sharyl 8, we spent four days with Fred in Vermont doing things that the children will always remember: Walking with Fred as he taught us who had made the tracks in the snow. Filling the suet and seed feeders for the finches, titmice, nuthatches, and cardinals. Holding up pieces of torn bed sheet between outstretched arms so the wind could send the children sailing on their skates over the frozen pond. And, of course, learning to keep the wood stove replenished from the stack of wood piled high on the porch. They knew that Fred, whose stature and bearded face resembled those of Paul Bunyan, had cut every tree and split every log resting there. And they also learned that the obligatory visit to "the aunts' house" was something people did as visitors to that small town, to make others happy.

Bruce realized very early in his adventure that the most important thing he brought to Africa was himself — who he is and where he came from.

Letters Home

November 10, 1981

Through

December 30, 1981

November 10, 1981

Dear Mom, Dad, Sharyl, Nerissa, Sparkle, & Anna,

I have arrived in Togo. The trip was stupendous. And what a surprise to find that David Apter had booked me first class on Air Afrique. I have enclosed one of the menus from which I chose my gourmet meals. The constant flow of French vintage champagne, vin blanc, burgundy, and cognac helped pass the 14 hours. Quite a contrast in riches compared to my introduction to Africa.

It seems like I've already seen half of Africa because we stopped in Dakar, Senegal; Freetown, Liberia; and Abijan, Ivory Coast, before arriving in Lomé on Tuesday morning. Getting into the city, my lack of proficiency in French cost me a $20 cab ride. No great loss though; it's about the only money I've spent, and I budget it under "learning." I'm sure my French will improve quickly.

Right now Apter and Associates has arranged for me to stay in a large suite in the four-star Hôtel de la Paix in Lomé. Last night my sleeping was screwed up with jet lag. I went to bed around 7 p.m., woke up at midnight, read for a while, back to sleep at 3 a.m., and then woke at noon. Adjustment has been facilitated by more gourmet cuisine and a constant strain of classical music piped everywhere.

It is <u>very</u> hot and humid, but that just means I don't have to iron my shirts. I really can't wait to get to the university. I'm dying to meet some people my age. I would love to play some basketball also. And I would especially like to get away from this high-class living.

· I went down to the city's beach today, figuring that would be a relaxing way to kill time until my meeting with the hotel manager. I thought it would be reminiscent of home and Ipswich. Far from it. The beach is gravel-like with brown-red sand and coconut trees all around. And the ocean doesn't seem like any ocean I've seen. There

9

is no transition where water meets land. It's ocean, then land. The water is as turbulent close in as it is miles out. The waves don't creep in and tumble ashore. They abruptly rise, peak, and crash. About 10 feet out into the water, it appears to be 20 to 30 feet deep. Not much for wading.

I will write you again soon.

I love you all,
Bruce

November 13, 1981

Hello Everyone,

All is great! I found my way to the Village du Benin, part of the Université de Benin, Togo's university. The village consists of a building where classes are held accompanied by a special lodging area for foreign students who have come to the university to study English. Most of the university buildings are of cinder block dorm/barrack construction. The village is slightly more upscale, catering to the higher expectations of the foreign nationals who bring with them valuable hard cash for their lodging rents. The village buildings are also of cinder block construction, but they are tastefully built in round bungalows where each room occupies a quarter of the circle. Residents at the Village include a Nigerian diplomat and a couple of members of the North Korean military who are stationed in Togo as advisers.

My room is great—big, screened windows, double bed, nice bedding, big fan, mosquito netting, closets, desk, two lounge chairs. I also bought a mat rug, a basket and a piece of African art depicting Africans rowing (!!)[1] and a lamp. I am well stocked, thanks to you all, and have almost everything I need. What I don't have, I will ask Apter & Associates to bring over on the travel writers' trip in December.

Adjusting to life at the university has not been that difficult. I have enrolled in a French class where I have met a diversity of foreign nationals studying here. The class includes a Russian diplomat's wife, some Korean and Chinese women, and a few Nigerians.

The food served at the village is not half bad. Every morning we get a large bowl of tea with lots of condensed milk and sugar—my

---

[1] *Bruce was on the rowing team at Harvard.*

kind of tea. Breakfast is 6:30 sharp, so I wake up at 5:30. For the other meals, I usually get a chunk of stew beef or a chunk of a large sardine-like fish. The cook just chops it in sections and cooks it. I never knew fish had so many bones. Then they serve you a humongous portion of starch, either farina, macaroni, rice, or yams, which here are like tough potatoes, with a very spicy sauce. Then we get a piece of baguette, a small bit of fresh vegetable with dressing, and either a citron—a cross between a lime and an orange—or a banana.

I drink incessantly, usually Sprite, Fanta, or Coke. Bière Benin, which is their local beer, is very good, and at about 10 cents a bottle, is cheaper than soda. The diet never varies much from that. When I'm doing some of my work while at the Hôtel de la Paix, I splurge and buy a liter of bottled spring water for $1.70. Here, if cars ran on water, it would cost more than gasoline.

Christmas presents do not look like a good idea this year. It would quadruple their price by my getting them to Apter and then his getting them to you. Plus it would be a royal pain to both us and Apter. I guess this will be our first truly small Christmas; [2] however, I feel like I have already gotten the greatest present of all being here in Africa.

The telephones are a royal pain. They are located in only a few wealthy homes and offices, the post office and hotels. What I will do is arrange with Monsieur Brown, who is the director at the Hôtel de la Paix, for a phone room where I can await your call at an appointed time. I think the 23rd of December would be the best time, and you must call me because it costs $50 a minute for me to call the U.S.

---

[2] *The family joke has always been to say we'll have a "small Christmas"— no big presents, no going overboard—and then end up having a huge pile of presents under the tree. Small, inexpensive gifts added to the fun of making it a "big" Christmas for everyone.*

Please call DA&A and tell him when you will call me, and then he will telex me. I will telex you the phone number as well as the telex number in case you can't reach me and want to postpone the call. That way I won't sit there all night waiting for your call.

Love you all,
Bruce

November 15, 1981

Hello Everyone,

This is the third letter I've written, and I still haven't received any mail from you. Please make sure I am on the church newsletter mailing list. Also, will you find out if Leslie Brown[3] at the *Ipswich Chronicle* was able to arrange for the paper to be sent to me?

I got a brainstorm today. If Don visits you after the 11th of December, I can get you Christmas presents from Togo. Someone from DA&A could leave them at the Air Afrique desk at Kennedy, where Don could pick them up. Write me if this is possible.

Dad, on my stopover in New York on my way to Togo, Don and I had a fun talk about architecture. It centered on discoveries, and how he used to thrill in discovering buildings, but he said he didn't get that same thrill very often anymore. He attributes it to age and a critical vein in him. We talked about the discoveries that I was expecting, how I might react, and how discoveries in Togo will have an effect on later discoveries in my life. Will it take a trip to the moon to match the thrill of this adventure? Or will it simply be a matter of discovering appreciation for an ordinary subject previously unnoticed?

As Don and I talked, we discussed African architecture. Don had been very excited by some of the things he had seen in books. I am going to ask him, and I ask you now, if you know of any architectural publications that might be interested in a little piece on an architecturally famous village in northern Togo called Tamberma. The houses in the valley of the Tamberma look like medieval castles, only they are made out of wood, sod, and mud. There is no other prototype or similar construction in the world. Let me know.

---

[3] *Editor of our local weekly newspaper.*

14

I'm anxious to get letters.

Love,
Bruce

Among the Tamberma, the thresholds of dwellings are always surrounded by an array of small fetish mounds.

November 23, 1981

Hello Everyone,

Everything is great. Very busy. Very français. Thanksgiving is two days away. I have been invited to eat at the Lerners', an American couple in their 50s. Gene Lerner is an engineer with the U.S. Agency for International Development (USAID) and his wife is from southern France. Their daughter is coming down from Ouagadougou, Upper Volta, and a few other Peace Corps and American Embassy people in Lomé have been invited. I have many friends of all sorts already.

One thing that I have been thinking about, and I thought I'd tell you about, is a dream that has recurred more than any other dream in my life. I have had the dream every other night since I got here. I have gotten to the point with my dreams that I will direct them as I please or realize, while I am dreaming that I am dreaming. But this exercise has only complicated the effects of this predominant dream.

The situations always change. Basically, I come home for some reason. One time, I was supposed to come to see David Apter; another time I flew home because I forgot something. Inevitably, when I get home, I realize that now I need another round-trip fare to return to Togo. Usually in the dream, David Apter talks to me and says there is no problem. But I feel unbearably uncomfortable being home, and I don't know what I should do. Say hello to people? The situation is awkward. In the end always comes the thought that I can't go back to Africa for some reason or another. Between the cost of the flight and its extensiveness, which you can only experience after having been en route for 24 hours, Africa seems forbiddingly far away. The dream always has different, nerve-rattling details, but those are the basics.

I'm not sure what motivates the dreams, perhaps a subconscious preoccupation with how far I am from home, only the dream views the contra positive of how far home is away from Africa. Perhaps it is repressed culture shock. Perhaps it's disbelief that all my dreams to come to Africa have come true. Perhaps it's a delayed-action manifestation of worries about not getting to Africa.

Whatever it is, it has gotten so strong that now I dream that I am dreaming these dreams. Last night, I dreamt that I woke up in my very own Village du Benin room after dreaming this dream, but the room was a bit different. I felt relief that it was only a dream; yet I was actually still dreaming. Then as I was fixing up my room, I was thinking of ways not to dream that again, when I was really awakened by another villageois calling me to breakfast. I hardly knew where I was then!

As I approach the end of my initial period of adjustment, I have been thinking a lot about security and insecurity. Two words that make the world go round. They seem to be the two key obstacles preventing peace on earth, and yet we know so little about them. I ponder them constantly and have caught only glimpses of their dynamics.

My Togo adventure has placed me face to face with security and insecurity. For a long time, I have thought of myself as an insecure person. Only now do I realize that I have been basically secure and that most of my insecurities were simply tensions, understandable confusions or ignorance. Now I think I am secure.

My thoughts, however, reach deeper than that realization. On this day I feel petrified, scared, lonely, and nervous. Insecure! So why do I call myself secure? Because my insecurity never goes beyond the emotional level. In other words, I don't allow my insecurities to dictate my actions. As a person living day to day, I am secure, yet I am still a person and not some automaton that does something without hesitation, just to follow orders or because I know I can do it.

I also think that marriage is a form of security, in that a mate can help insecurities stay actionless.

I await your phone call before Christmas.

Love,
Bruce

November 28, 1981

Bonjour Everyone,

I think this is going to arrive about Christmas. It's been a month, and I've received no mail from the States.

Everything is going well. My finances are doing well, and my bowels are doing well. I think I am rehydrated and know how to stay that way.

I am enjoying myself and am excited about what I do each day. I devour books. I brought around 7,000 pages with me, but that should only last a few months. I've always wanted to have this kind of time to read, and my French is getting a lot smoother too.

I really can't remember feeling culture shock except the first couple of days, and that could have simply been climate adjustment and jet lag. I think that my two-week trip to France in high school made a big difference. I felt much more tension then than I do now. I think my first experience abroad, absorbing vast differences, served as an inoculation to protect me for life. It's funny, just as I liked most in France the croissants and tea every morning, here I also love best their tea each morning. It is delicious served steaming hot with condensed milk and sugar.

I do, however, sometimes get very lonely. I cannot just pick up the phone and call someone. More, I am stripped of the normal relationships, in business, church, family. Also, my non-personal means of gratification are reduced, such as playing pinball, eating (especially at Elsie's and Bailey's,[4] and Hershey's with peanut butter), TV, music!!, card playing, Nerissa playing. I am left with reading, writing, resting, and exercising, all of which are wearing thin these days. Weekends are truly devoid of a chance to meet girls or set up a

---

[4] *Two Cambridge hangouts. Bailey's was known for its fantastic ice cream.*

date at this point. I still feel happy, excited, and calm, but also feel loss, loneliness, and yearning.

I did my laundry today. What a change it is from using the laundry facilities at the Phoenix Club. Instead of a few coins and a little time, I have two buckets, one for washing and one for rinsing. After pushing the clothes up and down in the bucket and rubbing them between my hands, then rinsing as best I can, I hang them up to dry. No hot water of course. But it works, and the dry air has them ready for me quick enough.

I had a terrific Thanksgiving meal. Because the Lerners have commissary rights at the embassy, they were able to procure a turkey and other delectables.

If you think the world is a small place, Lomé is even smaller. Work is very easy because contacts and information are so interlinked. It has been quite easy for me to get around as such and find new contacts. In my travels, I've been reminded of my junior high school trip to Williamsburg because there are so many similarities to what I see today in Togo. Comparisons such as children's games—hoops, primitive tiles and marbles, clapping, and kicking; cooking—over fires, well for water, spices prepared at home, open marketplace; make their own homes; status of cars/carriages; cottage industries—shoemaking, weaving, cabinetmaking, dressmaking; apprenticeships—painting, low pay; schools—use slates, cherish books, one-room schoolhouses.

I'm looking forward to the first travel writers' group arriving the second week in December. The group will include 14 American journalists, two Apter people who are lots of fun, and me. I will have a chance to debrief all the information I have accumulated since my first month here, which will be a great relief because it will show them for the first time how much I have done. Also, we will be able to iron out some problems I've encountered to facilitate and direct my future work. I will also get a chance to see the sights of Togo with them, while acting as their quasi-guide. It will be a treat staying at all the posh hotels, eating at the fanciest French restaurants and seeing the lavish jungle, game preserve, outlying villages, and other big attractions as I show them around.

Keep the letters coming.

Love you all,
Bruce

Bruce doing his laundry in wash and rinse buckets.

December 12, 1981

Hello again,

The group of travel writers just got here. Problems with the trip, but great to see and hear from everyone. I will be sending these letters back with the DA&A people on the trip, so I know you'll be getting them soon. Merry Christmas!!

Apter sent a Walkman over for me! Ecstasy!! If you can think of a way to send over your tapes and mine (in black box under my bed or in one of my closets) that would be a great (if late) Christmas present. Shipping rates I'm sure are too high.

Here is a list of bulky things I could use if you find an imaginative way to get them to me, i.e., someone coming to Togo. Books—any of my books, especially any of my books on West Africa, *Walden Two*, *A Distant Mirror*, *The Fountainhead*, *Born to Win*, *The Vast Majority*, or any you recommend. Also, my French Achievement Test Practice Book (bottom shelf of blue shelves) and any of my French novels, especially *L'Etrangère and Huit Clos*.

Also, if you are ever in Cambridge, can you go to the "Bookcase" bookstore, near Passim's? They have a good selection of used, cheap books. Look for any books on West Africa that would be useful for my research. English sources are rare here. Plus, I would like to keep what I use.

Those Halatore tablets expired January 1980. It's ok. I don't need them. I don't drink the water. I go through around seven to nine bottles of Fanta a day, but it costs me only $2 for all of them, at most.

You should see the sun here. It is Harmattan season. The Harmattan is a cold, dusty wind that blows from the Sahara in the north. Some days it's like a thick, red fog, which makes the sun look like a giant, brilliant harvest moon high in the sky.

Love,
Bruce

December 18, 1981

Hello,

The travel writers' trip just ended. You will have to excuse the sporadic change of thoughts in these letters. I've many things to write, but instead of mailing them, I figure they will get there more surely and quickly if I give them to Jack Sweeney at DA&A to send to you from Washington, D.C.

I just had the most extravagant, exciting week of my life. I stayed in five-star hotels in the paradise tropic spots of Togo and dined on the finest French cuisine in the company of world travel writers. I had escargots three times!

I have yet to receive ANY mail. The incoming mail system is highly suspect, so never send anything too important. David Apter is probably coming the beginning of January and can bring some mail with him.

Merry Christmas!! I've enclosed some things for you:

Sharyl. Thought you might like this African-style shirt. It's all they wear here. Save it for the summer. If you like it, they have other fancier ones in prints and batiks. These are more difficult to pick, so I thought I'd see if you like the style first.

Mom & Dad. Here is a set of what I thought would make super napkin holders. They are ebony models of the Asante "stools." The stools were comparable to thrones for the Asante Kingdom of West Africa. The capital was in Ghana, as well as most of its power, but the kingdom extended across Togo to Nigeria. The stools were thought of as more than thrones. They were actually thought to embody the very power of the Asantehene (king). When the colonizing British demanded the handing over of the "Golden Stool" (for the highest

24

king), it touched off a famous and ferocious war. You can find much more in the encyclopedia, as this system was one of the most famous in Africa. These stools are inlaid with ivory.

For everyone. A porcupine quill, which I found at the Lomé voodoo fetish market. The witch doctor told me that whoever has one of these in his possession will possess protection against all enemies, just as a porcupine has. Two quills were given to me in a village called Fazao (midcountry) by a boy whose picture I took with my Polaroid camera. I also took a picture of the chief as an official cadeau from David Apter, which overjoyed the chief. The boy gave me two quills, and then I saw them for sale at the marché fétishe. So I asked about their mystical powers and bought one for you.

For everyone. A travel fetish. This is the little guy with the mouth and the attached peg. You use it by taking the peg out of the guy's mouth, and then you whisper into the mouth that you would like a safe journey (by plane, car, etc.). Then, you must put the peg back into the guy's mouth to secure it. The witch doctor told me that it would be very bad if I, or someone who used it, deliberately took the peg out of his mouth during the voyage. However, if the peg falls out on its own, you lose your protection, but it is not bad for you necessarily, because it wasn't your fault.

I wish I could send more, but the other things that I think would interest you are considerably heavier. We will have a pseudo-Christmas in August for sure.

I miss the Season. David Apter & Associates have been great. Jack and Beth, colleagues from DA&A in Washington, came with the travel writers and, besides bringing my Sony Walkman, they also brought me a big Care package of toiletries, a typewriter and other necessaries, and everyone in the office bought me a Christmas card.

On the tour with the group, I really felt I was in Africa. We went on a safari and saw baboons, amazingly colored birds, an elephant, and many ibexes, deer, and gazelles. We spent a night at the Fazao Hotel, which was like an African chalet at which a James Bond vignette ought to be filmed. Then a bunch of us were sitting on the steps, chatting and drinking until the wee hours, when around two feet away, a tarantula marched right across the porch in front of us. This sure ain't Ipswich.

Just found out that it is best to write letters to Togo addressed "Togo, WEST AFRICA" or else one out of 20 letters gets sent to Tonga in the Pacific. It has been seven weeks and I haven't received a letter yet. I've lost faith in the incoming mail. Anything you have for me should be sent to Washington. Somebody from DA&A will be coming almost every month.

I got another gift for Mom, a Ghanaian brass bell.

Merry Christmas!

I love you all and look forward to your call on the 23rd.

Love,
Bruce

December 20, 1981

Dear Mom, Dad, Sharyl, Nerissa, Sparkle, Anna,

I went for a long walk and thought about something that might interest you. It's something that has been so much a part of our family, and certainly one of my more outstanding scripts— appreciation. It was what I considered a withered sense of gratitude through much of the wealth of experiences at Harvard that spurred this trip and adventure. Now that two months have passed, I have started to appreciate some things more, some things the same, and some things—to my surprise—not at all.

What I miss:
The first thing that comes to mind is ice cream. Big gobs of sweet, exotic ice cream with all sorts of goodies mixed in. Here they have simple, icy flavors served in bite-size amounts.

Cookies! Oreos! NutterButters! Fudge Stripes! When I think about it, I miss cookies when I'm eating cookies.

I miss girls. But I always miss girls, even when I don't miss girls. The socializing is very different here. The puritan ethic has been replaced by the 3000-Franc ethic. I haven't really gotten into that; I am looking more for some comforting companionship than excitement.

I miss cuddly things. Teddy.[5] Nerissa. Sparkle. I cuddle my pillow a lot.

I miss very close friends and warm conversations. I have not yet found a friend with whom I can really talk, and I do not have high hopes, in part because there are too many cultural barriers.

---

[5] *A tattered Winnie the Pooh that Bruce kept in his room from the time he was two years old.*

I miss the Phoenix Club, especially the convenience of things. The bridge games and the joking around. Not too much joking around here. Also not too much arguing. All the problems and answers are pretty clear-cut.

What I don't miss:
I don't miss classes, bills, my job at Harvard Security, looking for work in Africa, crew and other sports, the cold and snow, Whites, fashion, noise.

What I expect to miss when I leave Togo:
Control over every action and schedule. The peace! Long quiet walks. The friends I've made here.

One thing I've been surprised that I don't miss is Christmas. It is really hard to get into the spirit. Noel is just another holiday here. The supermarket has a bunch of cheap Christmas toys, and there are a few lights and decorations, but everything is in moderation. Even the old kicker—Christmas carols—are in indiscernible foreign languages. I think a few strains of the Nutcracker would do my nostalgia good.

Every day I feel more and more settled in. I am still accomplishing tremendous things for work, plus reading and discovering. The things I look forward to are the Apter trip in mid-January and the University of California students who will be moving in at the University of Benin soon.

Love,
Bruce

December 28, 1981

Everyone,

Despite the phone call, keep the letters coming. Many people have had delays with mail from the U.S. these past few months.

One thing I would like you to send me is interesting clippings from the papers, and please send me the church newsletter. I haven't received one yet.

I spent a very nice Christmas with the Lerners. Their daughter from Choate was visiting. I did, however, come down with a bad fever and spent a part of Christmas in bed. I'm feeling better now, but am running low on vitamin C, minerals, and protein.

I just got a letter that was sent December 10, and it was marked West Africa. So keep the letters (and packages if you desire) coming. The problem has been in Brooklyn, I think, where no postal worker knows where Togo is. I don't think we'll have any future problems with mail if you mark everything West Africa.

I wrote you earlier about appreciation and the things I miss. I don't know whether you noticed, but almost all of the things I miss are tastes and habits from university—1) the Phoenix Club. 2) Bailey's frappes (I don't miss the Dairy Queen). 3) convenience. Many a time the frig. and the cookie jar have been bare, and I could not just go to the Store 24. I fantasize so much about just going down to the Lowell House dining room to get whatever I want. 4) Food. Only at school did I eat to my heart's content with weekly gourmet meals at the Phoenix. 5) Music. At Harvard I was introduced to all sorts of music that I never really listened to in high school.

I had always subconsciously realized that since my initial plans, one of my main motivations in coming to Africa was to strip myself

29

of some of Western satiety and luxuries. Had I not gone to a place like Harvard, I don't believe I ever would have had the desire to come to Africa. In going to Harvard and joining the Phoenix Club, I got to see how the highest level lives. I was driven to Africa to see how the lowest socio-economic level lives. It was a motivating thirst for perspective that drove me to Africa.

With this new insight into my present feelings, I can guess what my future reactions will be. I think Africa will accustom me to freedom and living life as I see fit. I yearn to finish up at university, but I can see it being a good long time before I go back to an institutional framework of any sort.

I have tried to analyze my life now compared to my Ipswich days. The best way to describe it is that weekends and evenings are like our days in Vermont at Fred's place—reading at my leisure, writing letters, thinking, being in a relaxing, peaceful and gorgeous area. My days are like one big Student Advisory Board or Student Council project, hustling about the city, using my ingenuity, craft and people skills. Meeting with people, always toward an accord. Digging. I have even gone back to my old style of keeping a sheet of things to do each day, which I haven't done since my Ipswich High School days.

Vermont and Student Government have been, respectively, my ideal recreational and occupational settings. I have found them both in Togo. I will enjoy going back to the life of a Harvard student, but I will try to extract myself from many of my institutional responsibilities. I'm almost positive that I will forgo crew to pursue lifting and intramural sports. I am going to look for a job, not to replace, but to augment my Security job. Harvard Security is so good as a place of employment that I will probably never give it up. But I'm not sure I will be able to let it absorb me as it has in the past. On the other hand, the motivation to earn money may drive me to sign up for shifts as readily as before. I haven't changed that much.

I think a lot about what I will do after school. Not that I have any ideas. That's just it; I sit and contemplate the void that sits before me. The only thing I am sure of is that I want to start a family. I realize the danger of pre-convincing myself of this, but like everything, with a little help from my friends and a lot of help from you, I just know the perfect opportunity will present itself. I have had almost psychic feelings throughout my life about my future and what I should do. Some of my plans were, at times, against your desires or despite your fears, like adding Latin class to make an eight-class load in high school, football (your fear of my being injured), Harvard (your concern with costs), Africa (your fear of my going so far). In each case, I could not have fantasized a more spectacular result, a lot of it due to my foresight. I had been thinking of going to Harvard since my sophomore year in high school. Getting to Africa took over a year to accomplish. Marriage, I admit, is the toughest of all because my foresight, values, efforts and qualities make up only fifty percent of the picture, if that.

You may wonder how I could think of marriage when I just came off an almost fatal relationship and have zero relationships for the present or foreseeable future. However, deep down, I think you understand. Family has always been the focal point of my life, even when I was, and am now, far from home. Personal relationships are not only the most challenging, but also the most rewarding part of life, and these are at their apex in a family. In most ways, my life to this point has been basically self-centered. My goal has always been to make myself the best possible person to offer others.

My need for personal commitment and sharing seems to grow each day. I feel myself reaching "maturity," that point at which I feel that I am a person who can offer someone else guidance, warmth, security, and fun. I can see it in the near future, that is, after my graduation from Harvard. Everything from then on is a mere addendum of experiences, data, perspectives, color, and talents. Every day from then on that I can't share my life with someone to the fullest would be a waste. Not only my life then, but also my 23 years before.

I will look to you to protect me from myself. I have always vowed that the woman I marry will be someone whom you would love and adore as a daughter/sister. All Mrs. Lynns must be able to share as well as contribute to a trip to Vermont or a picnic at Bradley Palmer State Park.[6]

I look forward to your letters marked WEST AFRICA!!

Love always,
Bruce

---

[6] *A local park where families picnic, bike ride, and wade in the kiddie pool.*

December 30, 1981

Sharyl, Mom, Dad, Nerissa, Sparkle & Anna,

I got your first letter yesterday! It was great.

DA&A gave me another Christmas present—a moped. It really is necessary to get around. I sent him [David] a memo asking for an advance on my salary of $100 to $150 to purchase a moped, and the next day he cabled me $200 and told me to write it off as an expense. The two-wheeling is terrific. I beat all the traffic. The practicality and the driving involvement have me hooked.

I am now coaching the basketball team at the American International School (AIS) in Lomé, which goes up to the 8th grade. It's great fun. Nostalgia for Havlichek Camp days. We play the French School on January 20th. On my team is the son of the director of ECOWAS, which is the West African Common Market, headquartered in Lomé. I had already met him for an Apter assignment, and we hit it off as soon as he found out that I went to Harvard. He is a Harvard Law School graduate. Also on the team is the son of the assistant chargé d'affaires at the American Embassy, and also the son of the Nigerian ambassador to Togo.

Life is really starting to roll here. I'm pulling off a few real coups for Apter. I'm also becoming entrenched in the Lomé community. I see here the value of what I perceived at the Phoenix Club, that all real power and work come socially. The Phoenix Club and its weekly lunches and dinners accustomed me to political/business conversation, wit, manners and simple style. A confidence during a social situation does inspire confidence in others.

I eat dinner regularly at the home of Monsieur Brown, the director-general of the Hôtel de la Paix. Today, he had the vice president for African affairs for a West German steel company join us for dinner. Hans was telling me that his biggest problem is keeping down his weight because his business has made him a "professional eater." (The Lynns, Chadwick, and Wood should look into this!) It's just that business is often carried out over a meal; for fast-paced executives, it relaxes the tenor of affairs and allows work to be done at a time normally lost.

Hope to hear from you soon!

Love,
Bruce

II
Mosquitoes, Parades, and Funerals

The only way to make a difference with a boy is to give him powerful experiences that speak to his inner life, that speak to his soul and let him know that he is entitled to have the full range of human experience.

—Dan Kindlon and Michael Thompson,
Raising Cain

Each year our church spends three days as a church family at a retreat center at Ferry Beach, Maine. Bruce attended for many years and, as he got older, liked to join with the adults during the game-playing, music-singing, eating-too-much activities in the evening. We can calculate the stages of his and other church kids' growth, just as we can measure their height with marks on the wall, by their transitions from being told to stay at their parents' side, to going into a corner in groups to have their own fun, to wandering around the edges of the adult activities, to joining in games with the adults, to the stage during the teen years when they regroup and seem to disappear, showing up mostly for meals. One year someone taught us all to play Pounce, which is an adult version of Slapjack. Bruce loved it, and we knew he had grown that year into a new stage of hanging with the adults, which was not yet an embarrassment to him.

Bruce also loved his participation in high school football, which made autumn a special time of year for him. He played offensive tackle and defensive end under Coach Jack Welch, who is a legend in Ipswich and Massachusetts football.[7] Coach Welch was very adept at creating team spirit. His dad and I attended all of Bruce's games, but we especially remember the day his team won the state High School Super Bowl Championship.

The night before the big game, Coach Welch had the whole team check into a hotel near Boston University's stadium, where the tournament was to be held. He knew that having the team in one place, eating together the night before, then waking rested with plenty of time to get ready for the game, was preferable to hopping on buses that morning for the hour-long ride to the stadium. Welch's team was very ready to play that day. They went on to trounce the Newburyport High School team, which had previously defeated the Ipswich Tigers by one point during their only loss of the season.

In a football town like Ipswich, the winning team is held in high regard. In late afternoon on the day of the big win, the team rode from the outskirts of Ipswich back through town to the high school on fire trucks, whistles blaring. I had never seen Bruce so exuberant. Nor will I ever forget his jumping off the truck and lifting me off my feet, high into the air, to express his joy. He knew we understood how hard the team had worked for this victory, and how proud we all felt at that moment.

This American background must have seemed far away to Bruce when he lived in Togo, which is a tiny country shaped like an elongated triangle, dwarfed on a map of the enormous African continent. Bordered by Benin, Burkina Faso, and Ghana, Togo currently has a population of 3.9 million people, a total land area of approximately 22,000 square miles, and an extraordinary variety of ethnic groups who speak more than 40 different dialects. In the dominant dialect of Ewe, the word "to" means water and "go" means riverbank. The name Togo hence means "the edge of the riverbank." Despite the introduction of Christianity and Islam, the

---

[7] *William Pollack, in his book* Real Boys, *describes a coach as an "emotionally important figure in a boy's life whose role is to encourage boys to play cooperatively while nudging them away from attitudes that may make them self-serving, overly aggressive or even reckless."*

many ethnic groups have by and large remained animist, believing in totem animals, medicine men, soothsayers, and fetishes.

From European traders, especially those from Portugal in the 15th century, to the slave traders in the 17th century, and later to the Danes in the 18th century, the land known as Togo was visited and visited upon by various nationalities. France's protectorate power over parts of what is now Togo was soon followed by German domination. In 1914 the French and British invaded the territory and divided it. France received two thirds of the former German colony the part that is now Togo — as a mandate from the League of Nations.

Togo gained independence from France on April 27, 1960. In 1967 the army, under the command of 31-year-old Lieutenant Colonel Eyadema, seized power and abolished the constitution. Soon after, Eyadema pronounced himself president and outlawed earlier political parties; for many years he ruled Togo under a single-party system. Adopting a new constitution in 1992, and presidential and legislative elections in 1993 and 1994, Togo is in transition to multiparty, democratic rule.

The events experienced by Bruce in this small country started shaping his life as the months passed and a new year began.

Letters Home

January 2, 1982

Through

January 28, 1982

January 2, 1982

Hello,

I'm getting so annoyed about not getting your letters that I've started to dream about it. I dreamt the other day that all your letters came at once, and there were lots of packages. The packages were funny. Inside they all had rolls of toilet paper because you thought I would need it. But, at last, the prize package was that big box of homemade fudge Mom mailed in November. In the dream I was upset because it was store-bought and not your homemade kind.

Keep the letters coming. They'll get through. There must be some tie-up, because people tell me that they normally don't have any problem. The key is whether the letter gets stopped at the censorship office. Your letter did. It was all messily reglued.

I've gone through 4,500 pages of reading, and my speed is increasing every day. I'm paranoid about running out of reading material, but I'm at the mercy of whomever you can find from Washington going to Togo. Try to get some of my books and cassettes—my social life, education and free time all lumped together—down to D.C., so if someone from DA&A does go to Lomé, they are all set to bring them. I've already given you some ideas. The key is small print so I get the most books per shipping-weight cost. Here are some other ideas of books that you should find on my shelves: any Michener novel, *Crime and Punishment*, *Great Essays in Science*, and *A Theory of Justice* by John Rawls.

I'm running low on some vitamins. I think I told you that already. Your send-me-off Care package[8] has been vital. That white shirt was crucial. The vitamins are a real pick-me-up, and I think

---

[8] *As parents, we were most concerned about Bruce's nutrition in Africa, so we made sure to send him all sorts of vitamin pills.*

necessary with my diet here. Everything you thought of has been invaluable.

Happy New Year! It's Saturday night. I hopped on my mobylette and scooted about town, but nothing was happening, so I bought a moderate chocolate mousse at a small café to treat myself and went home. I'm to the point where I miss just milkshakes, and I dream of Dairy Queen blueberry shakes. Memories return to me from long ago of my protein power shakes, and of course the Bailey's chocolate malted frappes with an egg!

Things have been pretty slow over the holidays. A lot of people are gone. A lot of my favorite haunts, e.g. American Embassy library, are closed, and the embassy does not have its weekly movies on account of the holidays.

Life is very relaxing. Lots of reading and sleeping. On February 1st the six students from UCal/Santa Barbara start at the village, which is the next benchmark I'm looking forward to. Visitors from the U.S. are always a big occasion, especially since they will be peers and friends for several months.

One of the books I'm reading is an unabridged, modern language Old Testament, which, for all its influence and impact on people, I have never read through in its entirety. I'm on Numbers. That is one strange work! So far, I'm not too impressed with God or His Word. It probably gets better after the Pentateuch.

One of the biggest pains about not getting letters is that it makes writing them so much more difficult. I feel as if I have been writing into oblivion for over two months. I get no feedback, no answers, and no dialogue. Letter writing for me is half entertainment and half social life; that is to say, it is very important. I write around five pages a day. Over 60 days, that's been 300 pages, and I've received nine! A pretty one-sided conversation, if you ask me.

You should see these African kids. I've never seen anyone so aggressive or cunning. They constantly just smile and ask for "ten francs." Sometimes they just get down to brass tacks and demand ten francs. It used to be really obnoxious until I learned to play the game. I dig up some one-franc coins (worth around 1/3 of a cent), and whenever they ask for a "cadeau," or demand as the case may be, I give them one of these. They are never mad. They treat the whole begging thing as a game, and they obviously realize they've been beaten at it. Some really get into it and are quite good. You will see them briskly walking along in the distance, but as soon as they see you, they slow down, sometimes limp, and put on the most amazingly sullen faces, as if they are posing for a UNICEF cover, and say, "Monsieur. J'ai faim. Donne mois dix francs." (Mister, I'm hungry. Give me ten francs.) These types often persist as if in agony. I usually laugh at them, and then their friends start laughing, and they are quite humiliated at having failed.

It is amazing how my time here has altered my attitudes about charity and how it ought to be administered. So little charity actually gets to the people. The persons who really need it are apparent, and everyone, including myself, always gives them what we can. These little kids who have turned charity into a con game get quite repulsive, although I see many bourgeois tourists getting great satisfaction by freely giving the ten francs.

You have to come here to know the irritation of the native children's chant:

> "Yo-vo, Yo-vo
> Bon soir!
> Ca va bien?
> Merci!"

Rumor has it that the Germans taught this needling nuisance to the Togolese children for the express purpose of irritating the French right before France forced the Germans out of Togo after World War I.

Love,
Bruce

January 3, 1982

Hello Ipswichites,

There are some books I am dying to read. I really appreciate your efforts in looking for them for me. I have so much opportunity and desire to read. It's a great time to get a lot of reading done. The books will make my next two years at school much easier academically.

First, some books by Hofstadter. I may have some on my shelf, or you may have some at the church. Please don't get any others besides these; I already have read them if they are not listed here. To find: *America at 1750: A Social Portrait; America's Violence: A Documentary History; Anti-Intellectualism in American Life; Great Issues in American History, vol. I, From Revolution to the Civil War, 1765-1865, and vol. II, From Reconstruction to Present, 1864-1964; The Paranoid Style in American Politics and Other Essays; The Progressive Historians.* Also these other books, if you can find them secondhand: *The Dreyfuss Affair*, Guy Chapman; *The Odessa File*, Frederick Forsyth; *The Zimmerman Telegram*, Barbara Tuchman; *The Bible and The Sword*, Barbara Tuchman.

I'm getting a great tan and I've shaved off my moustache. I'll send you a Polaroid soon. I weigh about 194 pounds (lost seven pounds), but I'm in good shape. Mostly the bulk muscle weight came off when I stopped Bailey's frappes and weight lifting and started playing a lot of basketball. I can still do 40 pushups at a crack and 10 pull-ups.

My French is pretty much all set. I change from English to French with ease. Just need to add a little vocabulary, improve my grammar, and fine-tune my pronunciation.

After this year in Africa is over, I've got some big decisions to make about "real life," jobs, status at Harvard, etc. But the answer ought to come in December 1983. Things just seem to work that way.

Peace Corps is out of the question. I don't know whether I'd want to go abroad again. I'm going to have had enough of this monastic austerity style, so I won't be big on underdeveloped areas. I really don't want to go to D.C., but I realize my most obvious job opportunities might be there. Nor would I enjoy NYC for more than a year, but I may be forced there as well. I would like to try Chicago or San Francisco. Then again, I might like to do Paris, or learn another language in Germany, Madrid, or Moscow. England or Ireland offers no enticement to me. I'm sure I'll need and want to get away from New England again.

As far as where to start looking for a job, I'm sure I'll look into the UN. The Togo experience and French and Spanish could pull me along. I'm sure I'll take the Foreign Service exam and see what programs the State Department has to offer. I'm told the World Bank has a weak pre-professional program, so I will avoid that but keep my eyes open for any opening. Same with the International Monetary Fund. I will also probably interview with Berger and Berger. They are a well-known development firm, and if I don't find any attractive positions, at least I'd like to get my foot in the door for future prospects.

Graduate school is out of the question, although I will take the GMATs [Business School Aptitude tests] when I'm out of school. I think the dream option, which is not so far out of the question, is to finagle some sort of fellowship so I could do something interesting and have some freedom for about a year. Although many people are after the available fellowships, I think I would be a strong candidate. I will get my applications done early and see what pops up.

How did Sharyl do on her PSATs?[9] I remember that it was after I got my scores that I really buckled down to schoolwork and personal study. Sharyl, do you have a word of the day? How about a French word of the day? Mom and Dad should regularly ask you the French word for day-to-day objects. If you don't know them, you need to look them up. The onus is on Mom and Dad to keep it up. It is these day-to-day objects (food, furniture, parts of the body, articles) that are the blocks of speaking a language, yet I find them lacking so often in classroom French. Sharyl, make a point of listening to those Jacques Brel records, following the lyrics on the cover. Look up words you don't know. This is the French and European technique for learning the language—listening to American songs. It's a great way to ingrain pronunciation and fluidity.

You know it's funny. One of the things I've been trying to do in order to get over my nostalgia and withdrawal from such things as Bailey's frappes is to find new, convenient gustatory obsessions. I keep trying new pastry places and restaurants with moderately priced desserts. Usually the desserts don't entice me enough for me to want to get them again. Either I will run out of ideas and forget Bailey's in the process, or else I will be successful and overcome the haunting memories of malt that way.

Love to all,
Bruce

---

[9] *Preliminary Student Achievement Tests are taken by each high school junior who will be applying to colleges. When Bruce took his PSATs, he did well; however, he felt he could do better and wanted to do well enough to have his choice of schools. He decided that increasing his vocabulary would be the most helpful thing he could do before taking his final SATs, which are crucial for college admission. After a year of reading many word books, including the very popular Thirty Days To A More Powerful Vocabulary, he increased his English SAT score substantially. In the process, he got hooked on words. He has continued since his junior year in high school to learn a new word nearly every day.*

January 4, 1982

Hello Lynns,

How are you? I thought of you all today during conversations with an American Embassy official who is an old Peace Corps person from Togo, and with a businesswoman in African art, also previously in the Peace Corps in Togo. We were discussing how different the African attitudes toward death are from our own.

Young death is such a common thing. Not just of young children, but also of young adults. The embassy official recounted a typical story. A pregnant American, the wife of an embassy worker, was due to go on medical leave to the States for her delivery. About a week before her plane was to depart, and several weeks before she was due, she had premature contractions. She was forced to deliver in a Togolese hospital. Being premature, the baby died soon after birth.

The tragedy was that had she made it to the States, incubation facilities and standard U.S. medical care could have saved the baby. This was also heartbreaking for everyone at the embassy. However, all the Togolese couldn't understand the problem. They just assume that an early delivery means a stillborn child.

There is a great fatalism about death here. More than that, there is a great respect for death. The Africans here in Togo believe in ancestor worship, which means they have a great respect for the old and dying because they are the humans closest to divinity. They believe that when a man dies, he takes his place among the gods as a sort of adviser, and as the years go by, he becomes on a par with the gods. There are many sacrifices, and in Togo many fetishes to please the ancestors and to request and lobby for favorable weather and good crops.

Funerals here are very festive occasions, designed to celebrate the passing of a man or woman to divine status. There is endless music and dancing. It's like a big block party. I see them every night in Lomé. Also, because of the atmosphere here, there is commonly a lunar rainbow, a circle of refracted light around the moon at night. The Africans believe this "sign" is the deceased person on his way to an afterlife.

Dad, I just read in the paper about Danny Ainge playing for the Celtics. That must be the latest, big Auerbach coup. There must be a lot of hoopla about it. If he turns out to be everything they claim, the Celtics should be pretty unstoppable; however, the Sixers have been right above them for a long time. What are your feelings on the Celtics this year? Have the Sixers and Celtics met yet? How did the game go? What are the Sixers like this year? The same as usual?

Love,
Bruce

January 5, 1982

Hello Everyone,

Guess what! I found a whole group of Americans, the teachers at the American school and their families, who love to play Pounce, but they call it Nurtz. When we can find enough decks of cards, we're going to have a Nurtz party.

I think I told you about the Lerner family. I spent Thanksgiving and Christmas with them. Their daughter will be visiting Togo again on March 6. You can send any packages or letters to her in February, and she can bring them over.

You guys must be impressed with how much I'm writing. Just like when I was in France, it's my escape from French. Also, it's a good way to pass the evening if I don't want to look at traditional dance or hear about Togo's agriculture. I still haven't received any more letters.

Work is going great. I get so much done with my mobylette, and with basketball practice every day, I come home exhausted. It's like a farmer's life. I go to bed soon after sundown, around 8 p.m., and get up around 5 a.m. with the sunrise. Otherwise I get poor lighting.

You know, the mosquitoes haven't been bad at all. The big problem is that I don't feel them when they bite me, so I can't kill them. I don't think that affects the reaction afterward, but it certainly was satisfying at home to know I had destroyed the bugger that gave me the itch. Here I just see mosquitoes flying about every once in a while, but my body has a whole slew of itchy bites. I know that someone out there is responsible, but without catching them red-handed, I don't get the same satisfaction.

No malaria yet![10]

Love,
Bruce

---

[10] *The family joke has always been to ignore my various admonitions to the children to be careful. Bruce would often leave the house with "Bye, Mom, I'll make sure not to catch pneumonia, break my neck, or poke my eye out." His "no malaria yet" is a new twist on making fun of Mom's worrying about his health and safety.*

January 6, 1982

Family,

Finally! Two letters at once today! Mom's from November 30 and Dad's from December 6. It's quite funny hearing about things a month old.

Last night the temperature dipped into the 30s from the Harmattan, the cold, dry, dusty, northern wind.

Today I took sort of a break from my hectic work to sit in the American Cultural Center library. My obsession with words has served me well over the years. It helped pass the time when I worked at Crane Beach,[11] at my security job, and now here. I have also caught up on my reading the *International Herald Tribune*; it doesn't have Garfield.

I'm going to try to get a raise. In fact, if you talk to Apter, he will probably ask what you've heard. Say that I'm fine, I like my work, but finances are very tight. Out of my $100 a week, $70 goes to room and board. Since all my transportation expenses are picked up by Apter for my mobylette, I have nothing to pay for but soft drinks, laundry soap, occasional snacks on the street and the American movies. I've saved up around $200 already.

I love getting pictures. It's so nice seeing images of home. Also, some friends here gave me a photo album for New Year's Day. The French custom is to give New Year's gifts instead of at Christmas. They are called "étrennes." It was perfect. I brought a bunch of my favorite photos to Togo, and these friends always want to look at them, so their gift was very thoughtful.

---

[11] *Ipswich is known for this beautiful, expansive beach, once part of the estate belonging to the Cranes of plumbing fame. Bruce worked there two summers during high school parking cars and monitoring the changing rooms.*

I love the reports about Nerissa. I'm going to copy them and send them to Steve. Looking at Mom's photo, I've decided that my favorite season is autumn. It is so colorful and somber. I have very positive memories of autumn. Football. New school years. Thanksgiving. The autumn always holds new things, like Harvard, and I love new things.

Love to all,
Bruce

January 10, 1982

Hello All,

Things are going very smoothly. I'm really learning my way around. I'm starting to find substitutes for my cravings and desires, and I've discovered some good library resources. Please send all those books I've asked you for only if it is very convenient. I'm finding plenty of books here. I've also found some people with good recorders and music collections to keep my Walkman fed.

I had a checkup at the Peace Corps doctor's office, and I'm in fine shape. No amoebas, malaria, or parasites.

A couple of night ago I had a big thrill going to see James Bond/Roger Moore, in French—*Rien Que Pour Vos Yeux* (For Your Eyes Only).

Everyone here is getting psyched and prepared for Liberation Day on Wednesday, the 13th. The day is a big spectacle, similar to the one at Sadat's assassination. Air Force jets and helicopters have been screeching overhead for weeks practicing their maneuvers. The parade lasts for four hours, and the street has been blocked for as many weeks to make the grandstand preparations.

I'm starting to learn the native language here, which is Ewe, the dialect spoken by just one of about 50 different ethnic groups in Togo. A lot of fun.

Last night we had a three-team game of Pounce (Nurtz) with three teachers at the American School, one of their wives, and a Peace Corps volunteer visiting from up north. Also a lot of fun, but I do miss the luxury of the Phoenix Club and just dropping in to play a half hour or more of backgammon or bridge over light conversation, a coke and an Elsie's sandwich.

I'm starting to get into the Togolese street food in my search for substitute appeasements to the Lynn nemesis—snacking. I don't know what I'll do in the States without truly fresh oranges and bananas. The street vendors also sell bread made with a touch of sugar in their loaves, so it's like having freshly baked sweet rolls. The pineapple here is so sweet it is called sugarloaf. It is so tender that you eat the core, and you can eat a whole one without ever getting a hint of that acidic burn you get with Hawaiian pineapples.

I miss you all.

Love,
Bruce   .

January 13, 1982

Hello,

Happy Liberation Day! Today is the big national holiday. There was a big parade this morning. It was so interesting to see a small country like Togo express its national power. The event was very striking for all the Togolese, but for me it looked like a fancy suburban parade with more people than floats.

The people became the parade floats, with more petals and colors in their floral costumes than Donald Duck in the Rose Bowl parade. There were dozens of different groups, and each had its own costume of special, colorful Dutch prints. It was like seeing all the bolts of Dutch cloth in the Grand Marché materialize into a smiling, singing crowd. This cloth is a big item here, as well as being very attractive. Each little regiment of people was wearing ornate, identical African-style dresses or outfits. Most wore elaborate floral designs, the effect of which was not unlike the Rose Bowl parade.

I guess the word that comes to mind for this day is quaint. The parade was next to the sea, so Togo's navy—two armed cabin cruisers—gave a 21-gun salute. They had an air show by Togo's Air Force—five planes and a helicopter flying straight ahead a couple of times. Then, the president's "Air Force One" commercial jet flew over for effect. I guess the epitome of quaintness overcame me when the High Commission for Tourism "regiment" passed by. Basically, all the bellhops from the hotels came by looking as spiffy in their uniforms as the Green Berets.

Then all the sports teams passed by. They were quite sharp; their sports uniforms were colorful and dazzling, very reminiscent of the Olympics. But the "sports" were something else. Did you know Togo has a national horseshoe team? It was followed by the table tennis team, each one marching with paddle held firmly in hand, as were the horseshoes. President Eyadema passed by the clapping onlookers in nothing more than a jeep. The doors of the jeep were taken off to expose even his feet to the gawking throng. Crackpots and turmoil are not known here it seems.

There were probably 50,000 marchers, which struck me as pretty funny for a country of 2.6 million people. Can you imagine that percentage of the United States population in a parade for the bicentennial?

Nonetheless, the parade in all its diminutiveness was tremendously impressive. At the end, all the different tribes of Togo—there are many—sent their 30 best folklore specialists to the parade. For about an hour, there were dozens of natives dancing, chanting, costumes, ornate masks, intricate rhythms, infinite noisemakers, foot stomping, all having a good time. It was a marvelous chance for me to see some of the more arcane native folklore, which doesn't condescend to descend on the tourist crowd. That part of the parade was as resplendent as it was exciting.

Love you all,
Bruce

January 15, 1982

Hello everyone,

One of the things I have had a real opportunity to do is look at some of the issues of developing countries. I'm going to be sure to take a course on development economics at Harvard next year. One issue I've gotten a lot of insight into is the Nestle boycott.[12] The whole debate misses most of the really important points, both pro and con.

Most of the proponents of the boycott claim that 1) Nestle is responsible for deterring breast feeding by pushing powdered milk on women in hospitals, and 2) Nestle "dries out" the mother in the hospital (she stops lactating when she stops breast feeding), and the mother is thus "hooked" into further use of Nestle, and therefore 3) the baby is fed with milk made from impure water supplies.

First of all, Nestle is only one of many dozens of powdered milk companies that sell here. Powdered milk is a very common and competitive product. Fresh milk just isn't feasible, and milk and dairy products are needed as part of a balanced diet. Dried milk keeps very well for long periods of time without refrigeration; not many foods are like that, especially protein sources.

Second, the drying-out issue is not entirely contingent on the introduction of powdered milk. Because of the extended families here, very often a mother doesn't take care of her own child, especially if she works, but a non-lactating aunt or grandmother does, which can cause the mother's own lactation to stop anyway.

Third, the water here is <u>not bad</u>. It is all they have. Humans have been living on worse for eons. Drinking water is very rarely a real problem. Because it is so vital to existence, governments prioritize it on their list of infrastructure development. With the modern

---

[12] *Twenty years ago, the boycott was big news in the United States.*

technology of wells, plumbing, and water filters, water is rarely a day-to-day problem. Since it can be an extremely hazardous situation if anything does go wrong with the water, given its importance, this often gives a misguided view of the day-to-day danger of third world water supplies.

On the other hand, I have found out that "drying out" is costly for another reason. A woman who is lactating is considered infertile, thus hyperextended lactation is a common form of natural birth control, which has been accepted, mastered, and practiced traditionally for ages around the world. So, dry milk propagation can have a deleterious effect on low birth rates, which are so key to development.

My feelings overall boil down to a basic dilemma in development philosophy. On the one hand, there was a native, traditional system of prolonged lactation that provided a safe and steady supply of infant nourishment as well as a form of birth control. Really, the only birth control here is being pregnant. I've never seen so many pregnant women. African clothes make great maternity outfits because half the time that is how they are needed. On the other hand, the big, modern West came along and offered dried milk. Mothers ate it up, so to speak, and it did, in general, improve the health of infants. I'm convinced of this. It also freed up the women to be more productive economically. In the spirit of the yin and yang, we are faced with looking at development with many good qualities, but at the sacrifice of a heritage of equilibrium.

My personal view is that once modernity hits an area, there is no turning back. This new kick in development for "traditional method improvement" is merely a roundabout way of achieving modernization through different means. The ends are the same— technology, Coca-Cola, money, cars, stereos, pictures, and more food; therefore, I don't think the powdered milk market will be able to extract itself, even if it wanted to. It is a fait accompli, much like the mother who has dried out.

I realize also that the catalyst behind the Nestle boycott was the claim of unfair marketing practices—price gouging, price differentiation, medical kickbacks, misleading advertising; however, Nestle is no monopolist of underhanded marketing, even if it is guilty. If that were Nestle's sole crime, it would only be consistent to boycott most of the mass-produced products of international companies in the world today. Since that is not possible, we must rely on the law enforcement agencies, however ineffective, especially in these small nations.

What the boycotts are really against is the adverse effects of modernization. I hesitate to say that they see a half-empty glass of milk that is also half full. Certainly, I do not believe it fair to punish only Nestle for such a crime. International Harvester, Sony, and Marlboro cigarettes have committed far more enormities. Regrettably, be it the inexorable path of human events or cruel human nature, in the end I take a very positive, accepting attitude toward development and modernization. For example, with Western powdered milk must come Western birth control. I hesitate again to say it, but it is no use crying over spilled milk.

Love,
Bruce

January 18, 1982

Hello Everyone,

Dad, I don't know whether you ever poked around in my *Gödel, Escher, Bach*, but while I was reading in the American Cultural Center, I came across the enclosed article in the latest *Scientific American*. It is delightful reading and gives a good flavor of the theme of the book. The "self-reference" philosophical question was one Gödel made outstanding progress in. Gödel is known for his "Incompleteness Theorem," which is thought by many to be the most important theorem in all mathematics and philosophy. He essentially says that whenever man finds any comprehensive code of physical laws, mathematical theory, logical system, elaborate computer program, philosophical dogma, etc. that claims to "explain" or "account for" <u>every</u> phenomenon in the universe, <u>there will be at least one inconsistency</u>. Hence, or else, for a "system" to be consistent, it must be incomplete (thus the name).

This theorem has thrown a monkey wrench into the work of mathematicians, philosophers, logicians, computer programmers, and the like for more than 70 years. The theorem denies them their raison d'être—that is the "ultimate" answer or the ULTIMATE TRUTH. That is why Hofstadter ties Gödel to Zen in his book, because the latter also attests to the elusiveness of final truth. Gödel "proves" his theorem through an elaborate, comprehensive mathe-logistical schema reminiscent of these "self-reference" dilemmas in Hofstadter's article. Half of one whole course at Harvard, the follow-up to my logic course, is spent going over Gödel's proof, the parts of which are much more sophisticated and abstract than the word games presented here.

I hope you enjoy the article. It is a good introduction to the concept of the book, so you might want to follow it up by browsing at some chapter. I recommend reading the parts that talk about Zen because you are familiar with that philosophy and his analogies and connections might become clearer. The whole tie to Bach and Escher is more evident in this article. Bach's arias and constantly rising canons have the same musical structure as the sentences in this article. Hofstadter looks at the musical dilemmas and self-referential repetitions in the book. Also, Escher sort of does in a two-dimensional medium what these sentences do. Paradoxes of dimension and planes rather than meaning and reference. Finally, I would greatly appreciate your going to the library to get his column in the January 1981 *Scientific American*, which he refers to in this article.

Everything is going terrifically! My mobylette is now working well, so I'm scooting about everywhere. I go to the American School a lot on weekends and get a weak but nostalgic hot shower and look up words in the air-conditioned library. We have Nurtz nights twice a week. Last Saturday we had five teams. Memories of Ferry Beach.

I had my inaugural accident on my mobylette when I hit a patch of sand. I got banged up, but not really hurt; however, the mobylette lost a muffler, a pedal, and an axle. Getting everything back in working order was more of a pain than anything else. The mobylettes are just like some people. They're an endless source of frustration, never work when you want them to, and are indispensable to daily living.

Still no more letters, which is quite frustrating. I've mailed letters to 19 people and have only received three from you and one from Grandma and Grandpa.[13]

I'm doing a lot of research these days, and I'm really pleased with the results. I'll have Apter send you copies of my articles. I've done a lot of research on and at the National Museum. One artifact exhibit really fascinated me—the "FA-DU." The FA-DU is essentially an oral

---

[13] *His paternal grandmother, Edna Lynn, and grandfather, Charles Lynn.*

tradition I-Ching. They have two strings of four half shells of nuts. They "throw" the strings and the shells land either facing up or down. Each pattern of up-down-up-etc. is its own named FA-DU, which has a rather arcane proverb associated with it. Each of the eight shells contains 256 proverbs, two to three sentences long, to be remembered in this oral tradition.

KDOY-N (good-bye in Mina, another southern Togo dialect)

Love,
Bruce

January 19, 1982

Hello Everyone,

Yesterday, George Brown at Hôtel de la Paix shared with me some interesting facts about African architecture. When huts are built in Togo, within the fresh composition of the clay and wood are termites and other organisms that fight and consume dangerous bacteria and germs. After a while, these organisms "eat" all of the germs in the household while the termites work their way through the wood. Thus, an old house in time becomes an unsanitary one. Because of this "organic architecture," Africans have adopted a "throw-away" mentality with houses. Instead of regular maintenance, which could not replenish those symbiotic organisms anyway, they do makeshift hack jobs on weathered parts of the house, figuring they're going to have to build an entirely new one eventually.

M. Brown explained to me that when the durability and sterility of modern technology and architecture came along, this old mentality was hard to drop. Africans in Togo just don't have a sense of maintenance, not to mention preventive maintenance, and such an idea is difficult to teach.

I find it difficult to figure out what's true in Togo. Basically, if you hear it twice, it's true. Several people have told me that the Togolese think it impolite to say that they can't do something, so they always nod an affirmation in reply. However, there is supposed to be some sort of tacit understanding through the voice inflection and demeanor that makes it very clear among the Togolese when something that you've brought in for a repair, for example, will be ready. I get the feeling that the Togolese don't ask, they just keep coming back, at their convenience, until something is finally ready.

There is another seemingly related instance of this "insult-in-asking" phenomenon. Most Togolese are insulted when you ask them if they want a drink. Good Togolese hosts just bring out refreshments. David compared it to someone coming up to you asking if you want a Christmas present.

Another pensée on cultural understanding. I was thinking of how much flak Togo and tightly, centrally controlled governments get for reporting "99%" tallies on national elections. We see this as rigging and suggest such to the rulers who will usually win by a majority anyway. They are used to needing a consensus, often coming from areas (Africa, Latin America, and Asia) where leadership is not elected, but decided collaboratively. Culturally, to them, it is the way that things ought to be presented. If the silver spoon were in their mouth, our advice would be analogous to their telling us that Reagan should have fudged his winning figure so his country would not have a questionable government of a slim majority. But the bottom line in all these things is that with Coca-Cola, Sony, and wheat come the Magna Carta and all the Western legal concomitants.

Love,
Bruce

Bruce with an acquaintance from the university.

January 20, 1982

Hello Everyone,

I got your November 30th letter today, a little less than two months old. Thanks so much for all the stuff you sent with the letter. A letter really makes my day; in fact, my whole week. Still no sign of the Christmas package you sent, although I think some censorship official has eaten well. I've no real hard feelings, though. I've returned the letter's envelope so you can see what censorship looks like. The letter inside was stuck with glue to the envelope. The crowning insult or joke, however you take it, is the stamp on the back "parvenu en cet état" (received in this condition).

I get a kick out of it, but watch what you say. Notice the red squiggle on the stamp. That's an African signature. Everyone has some sort of hieroglyphic, arcane squiggle with which they sign all documents, checks, etc. They've supposedly licked the problem of forgery because each person develops curves and idiosyncratic twists unique to his writing, unlike script writing where we are taught a fairly uniform form. So, Dad, if you ever come to Africa, you may find one place in this world where people will not look askance at your signature.

Also, interestingly, in Togo you don't give someone the finger; you give them the whole hand! Kind of looks like giving someone the "whammy." Roughly translated, the gesture means "yourmotha."

As I read the questions in your letter, I realized the problem of this time lag in correspondence. Some of the questions about food, etc., I have talked a good deal about already. Nonetheless, here are some quick responses.

Yes, I'm starting to eat more "street food." My system has adjusted. I'm drinking the water, filtered, and my amoeba phobia has dissipated. Street food never costs more than a quarter.

Here are some of my favorites:
Togo-Do-Nuts, which are homemade, little fried dough balls that cost three cents apiece.

Peanuts, either sugarcoated or dry roasted. They are prepared in someone's home and are really fresh. They sell them in old whiskey bottles for $1 or $2. I love eating peanuts and fresh bananas together. Bananas are three for ten cents. I don't buy the candy-coated peanuts much because I can't stop eating them.

Fried plantains, an African specialty. A plantain is like a large two-foot-long banana but less sweet. They fry them, and they taste like sweet potatoes, which I never liked.

Oranges, as sweet and juicy as you can imagine, and they cost only 14 cents for two.

Fried yams, which are like steak fries, but less sweet. They are fried like french fries but they are tougher.

Lastly, there are the turkey tails. These things are famous. The Togolese import these turkey tails from the United States. Peace Corps friends tell me that Togo is the sole market in the world for these tails, which are fatty turkey flesh and delicious. They cost 37 cents apiece. There are so many turkey tails here that I read one short article noting that Britain is going to try to start exporting their turkey tails to compete with the U.S.!

I'm now eating at a different cafeteria at the university. It is much cheaper because it is government subsidized. Also, I can eat with more francophone people and meet more Togolese. At the other cafeteria in the housing village, most of the students are foreigners like me. Their menu is pretty much the same as I have described to you before.

I also like eating street food because it is an incentive to learn Mina, since most of these ladies don't speak French. I've also learned how simple the dynamics of language-barriered communication can be, especially in commerce. I just point to what I want, hold up as many fingers of the item as I want, and she responds by showing me the coins necessary to pay for it.

In answer to your other question, no, unfortunately there are virtually no telephones here! Anywhere!! Except hotels, ministers' offices and the post office.

Love,
Bruce

January 22, 1982

Hello Family,

I've enclosed a postcard that shows Kente cloth, the artistic gem of Africa. The fabric combines very rich threads of many bright colors, as you can see on the card. It is sold in large pieces, like the woman on the card is wearing, but those cost hundreds of dollars. They also come in strips around six inches wide and as long as you want. The large sheets are just a lot of strips sewn together. The strips would make a colorful wall hanging or runner, but I can't think of an appropriate place in the house for you to hang one. If you think of a place, let me know and I'll pick up some fabric for you.

Today was very exasperating. But if it had gone totally all right, then the week's success would have been almost too much to believe. I've had a very good week, and it was topped off today by my going out to participate in native Togolese fishing. I actually went out in the ocean in a tiny 15-foot dugout canoe, paddling with canoe paddles, laying the net down, and then pulling it in to the tune of "A-Hay-Ho!" I think the fishermen liked the way I really participated and took a sincere interest in the work. It was fascinating.

I got a tremendous article out of it; however, the pièce de resistance was my action photos of fishing out in the water. I think they are the first ever done! BUT, as I was about to rewind the film, I hit the "open" button by mistake. The back of the camera popped open a bit. I was devastated! I immediately shut it, but I fear the damage has been done. However, all the good pictures were in the beginning. If light didn't get in and ruin the roll completely, I will be endlessly happy.

I have decided to adopt two apothegms for each day. One is: Happiness is a purring mobylette," and the other is actually two mottos that guide my every action: "All things come to those who wait" and "Carpe diem—Seize the day!" To be able to coordinate both is a dexterous feat with unimaginable results.

Love,
Bruce

January 26, 1982

Dear Mom, Dad, and Sharyl,

I have started to realize the value, as well as the values, of African business. Togo may be more advanced in the labor movement than the Western world. Between funerals, birthdays, Muslim, Christian, and state holidays, they have accomplished a four-day workweek. The Africans have taken laissez-faire philosophy to the extreme; they don't interfere at all in the economy, least of all by going to work or promoting their own business.

The attitude of missed appointments, arbitrary closings of places, and slow service used to peeve the very organized, business-minded me. I used to get bugged at Mr. Owebo, who ran the "burette," or local concession stand on campus. Many times after a basketball game in this very hot climate, I really wanted a cold drink. I'd make the mistake of expecting the stand to be open, being the middle of the day.

So many times it was closed or Mr. Owebo had just stepped out and closed up shop. I cursed him endlessly each time and mentally grouped in some of his culture-mates in my personal vituperation. I never vented this anger, however. It seemed as though just when I'd expect it would be the last time on earth the place would be closed, there it would be, locked up tight. I wasn't the only one frustrated. I would find many a student upset, turned away or anxiously waiting for it to reopen.

Only this past weekend have I forgiven Mr. Owebo his idiosyncrasies. On Saturday I was laid up with a bad case of dysentery and a fever of 104 degrees. He heard about this and right in the middle of a hot day, when his business was the hottest, he decided to close up shop, come to me, wish me "du courage" and give me two free cokes.

69

It was about the dumbest, most economically unsound thing he could have done. Adam Smith would have cringed. Yet it was the most human thing anyone could have done. I had actually been dehydrating from a combination of diarrhea and fever, and I had been dying for a drink. It is this humanity which screws up all of the economists' equations, lowers the GNP [gross national product] figure and puts Africa under the label of a "backward" country. I wish some Americans I know were a bit more backward.

Love,
Bruce

January 28, 1982

Sharyl, Mom, Dad, Nerissa, Sparkle, & Anna,

In a couple of hours I'm going to go pick up your Air Afrique package. I'll finish this letter after I get it.

Our basketball game was a great success. It was the highlight of the American community for a long time. The rematch is February 10th. There were little cheerleaders in uniforms and cheering parents. It really was thrilling. It was funny being the coach. The 4-5-6 graders lost badly, 10 to 40, but the big game against the 7-8 graders was won in a hair-raising, spine-chilling, throat-hoarsening defensive duel of 21-20. It was fun arguing with the referee in French.

I have enclosed the write-up of the game that I wrote after for the school. The *Post-Game Gazette* is a vestige of my 8th grade days with Peter McClelland, my teacher and basketball coach who used to do a game summary for our team. I'm going to send him a copy of the game write-up. He did a lot for me in 8th grade. He got me to Havlicek Camp and actually taught me my first unit ever on Africa. The team is a great source of pleasure for me. I work so well with the kids that they've asked me to be a substitute teacher ($50 a day!). That will be exciting. I'll write you after my first day in the classroom.

Related to your questions, there is no need to send another package, but if you do, here are some things to put in the Care package—nostalgic treats—use your imagination. I still haven't gotten Mom's fudge. Books you really recommend. At this point I have no preferences because I have uncovered so many sources of books. Voice cassettes of you all, maybe around the dinner table, maybe at one of your fun parties with the Bertellis, Buddenhagens and Eameses.[14] No medicines. I'm all set now. Thanks.

---

[14] *Close friends in our extended family.*

71

Also, can you send me copies of those two Nerissa pictures so I can send them to Steve? I love the black-and-white family photo, and I do enjoy getting the church newsletter a great deal. You know what else would be enjoyable? Receiving a tape recording of a particularly interesting church service. A sharing service would be especially enjoyable.

I'm listening to Pachelbel now as I write, and the crickets outside are trying to keep up with the violin crescendo but are falling asynchronously behind. I feel like I'm in some Vermont hideaway on a summer's evening. I think you've got to love life to live it.

Earlier today was quite hectic. Again, the mobylette. This time, just after I went through the hassle of getting my package, my carburetor snapped—10,000 francs ($37) and three hours of hassle at the peak of my excitement. (DA&A will pay the bill.) I had to pay 3,200 francs ($12) import tariff on the Care package because they said I could possibly sell the cassettes. C'est la vie.

Keep the letters coming. Some day they will all shove through in a blitz of greetings. Write whenever you get bored, stream of consciousness stuff. Nerissa reports are great.

I'm looking forward to February. It should be a much more relaxed, controlled, personally satisfying month. I'm also looking forward to it for another reason. Before I left D.C., the Starkeys[15] gave me a 1982 Snoopy calendar as a going-away present. It was the first and, for a long time, the only wall decoration in my simple room. However, for three months (Nov, Dec, Jan), I've had to look at the same January design; therefore, seeing a new month's picture will be a big event.

Thanks so much for all your consideration. You looked so handsome in the pictures. I've shown all my friends the pictures of

---

[15] *More family friends.*

the family. Sharyl, you have six marriage proposals if you ever want to move to Africa. You are really getting stunning. With all the clothes you got that first 45 minutes of Christmas, you won't be able to hide any of your good looks.

I love and miss you all.
Bruce

POST-GAME GAZETTE[16]

American International School—January 28, 1982

Opening days are always full of excitement and tension, but I have never seen one as heated as this one. The spirited cheerleaders looked sharp. Marie needs to make one more skirt for our new honorary cheerleader, Mr. Vasquez.

The key problem of the day was having only one referee. He did do a good job considering the emotion, confusion, and action of the game. All future games will have two referees, however, to keep the physicalness down and keep the game "du calme."

Special congratulations go to the board keepers Joumana and Nanette, timekeeper Angella, and official scorekeeper Laurie. I think they were the only ones who kept their heads in the tumult. Thanks to George for his special help and excellent job in keeping statistics and record for me on the play of the game.

FINAL SCORE:
AIS: 21   French School: 20

Team Statistics:

	1	2	3	4	TOTAL
Turnovers	2	4	0	5	11
Rebounds	6	5	11	3	25
Assists	4	0	0	3	7
Points	13	2	4	2	21

---

[16] *Bruce's calling on the influence of an 8th grade teacher's game summaries in his first coaching experience proves to me once again how important dedicated teachers are. Bruce's post-game summary shows how proud he was of each team member.*

Individual Player Statistics:

	Turnovers	Rebounds	Assists	Points
Hung	-	5	1	4
Joe	4	3	1	4
Nyema	1	9	2	2
Trip	3	4	2	9
Anthony	1	-	1	2
Nancy	-	-	-	-
David	2	-	-	-
Brukhardt	-	2	-	-
Claudia	-	2	-	-

Trip started the game off like there was no tomorrow. And soon it seemed as if there would be no tomorrow. When the French realized they could stop with brute force that which they could not stop with their skill, they started the barrage. The ref did not interfere, and the rest is history. The rest of the game was as painful emotionally to watch as it was painful physically to play.

Joe hustled and bustled and threw in a shot from somewhere near the Hotel Sarakowa. Hung and Nyema dominated the key at both ends, always in there for the key rebound or pass. Anthony gave great relief from the bench. David kept up the team spirit and tempo. Burkhardt never played basketball as well as he did this game. Claudia made perhaps the most unexpected clutch plays of all. Nancy seemed to play better with each minute she was in the game.

Joe's hustle is good, but the French defense was better. They stopped him legitimately by double-teaming. The court was small and the opponents were big. One cannot dribble out of those situations. It is a shame that we could not take advantage of our speed. They played a wise, dribble-stopping, double-teaming, frustrating press suitable to their size advantage and the small court. The way to break a press is with fast, accurate passes and MWB

(Movement Without the Ball) to the open spots. If there are two—sometimes there were three and four—players on Trip or Joe, SOMEONE is wide open for an easy shot, or should be. If you are open, yell it out, or mention it to the guards when the play stops. If you are not open, get open.

Nyema's practice problems came to haunt him: too slow, too lackadaisical, poor passes, poor concentration. Hung needed some stickum. Nancy has to stick to her opponent on defense and grab the ball—don't swat at it—on defense and offense. David and Burkhardt should hold up the ball and pass it when they make their good defensive steals. They are not master dribblers, and even master dribblers would have had problems dribbling through the mess out there of swinging legs and arms. Anthony has to get open more and hustle to spots that will be good for getting passes. He's got good hands, good shots, but they're worth nothing to the team unless he can get the ball.

Overall, the game was won with our scrambling defense, for which everyone deserves credit. The big problem and mistake were having only one referee. All future games will be remedied with two refs, so there will be more fouls and penalties called (at least twice as many) and more control of the two teams. The game was not ordinary in its officiating or level of physicalness. But extraordinary games and situations constantly arise and it's up to the classy ballplayer to keep his or her head and keep playing for the hoop.

Do not (Nyema and Trip) make pleas to the ref during the action. Many times you let up to complain about no foul called. Even if your claim was just, the smart French players stole the ball and marched down court on you. Keep playing no matter what. Our goal is to put the ball in the hoop. If someone has something to say to the ref, wait until the whistle blows. And, if someone has something to say to the opponents or their spectators...write them a letter! I don't blame anyone's high emotions; however, I was not pleased with what some players did with those emotions.

76

Congratulations on your first victory.

GAME AWARDS:
Most Valuable Player: Trip
       Offensive Standout: Hung
       Defensive Standout: Joe
       Unsung Hero: Claudia
       Sixth Player Award: Anthony
       Most Impressive Personal Game: Burkhardt
       King of the Boards: Nyema
       Best Spirit: David
       Most Improved Performance: Nancy
       On-The-Floor, Dave Cowens Purple Heart: Trip

Bruce coaching the American International School basketball team.

III
Old and New Cravings

*The capacity to use language, to tolerate distress,
to show and name feelings, and to be timid or eager
to explore are all dramatically affected by the
emotional environment created for a boy
during early childhood. While nature creates boys
whose behavior is influenced by biological
proclivities—more than we used to believe—nature
also creates boys who are more receptive to
interaction with their caretakers than we had ever
imagined.*

—William Pollack, Real Boys

During our parenting years, Ed and I seemed to know intuitively that even when they didn't show it, our children were receptive to our interaction with them. They were listening even when they pretended not to be.

Ed's father, Charlie, an Irish immigrant who married an English immigrant soon after they arrived separately in this country, nurtured his son from early childhood. Ed remembers him as a man of fine character who, through his service to his church, Boy Scouts, and the Masons, taught his two sons caring and integrity. Charlie also did each task with excellence, attaining the highest rank of Silver Beaver in scouting, as well as the highest rank in the Connecticut Masons. But the message he gave to Ed, who was working to become an Eagle Scout, was that building character was more important than the badges one could accumulate. Although Bruce never showed any interest in becoming a Boy Scout, his grandfather passed on to his grandson the same emotional environment of nurturance.

In our family, the parent of the same sex seems to have wielded the greater influence on each child's ability to explore the world with confidence. Bruce and his father also shared the wry sense of humor that manifested itself in Ed's letters to Bruce from, or about, his cat, Nerissa, which were usually signed with a not-too-real-looking paw print. In the Lynn household, Bruce's cat had assumed an air of superiority over our dog, Sparkle, and our cat, Anna. His father captured this back-home dynamic very well in the anthropomorphic "Nerissa letters," which Bruce loved receiving so far from home.

Here's a family favorite:

FOR SALE: Cute kitty cat that answers to the name of Nerissa. You will adore the way she rolls over and stretches out on tables. Call and ask for Anna. Don't talk to anyone else. Will sell cheap.

Dear Bruce,

Wow! That was close. As I was going out to the church yesterday with several letters to mail, Anna asked me to drop off a letter to the Want Ads magazine. I said sure. Then on the way to the post office, it suddenly hit me, Anna's never asked me to mail a letter before, so why is she starting now? I decided to take no chances. What could she be selling? All she owns is a cat dish and a scratching post.

I opened the letter and you can see what I found. Yes, Anna was actually trying to sell Nerissa, your cat! Well, you can be sure I didn't mail the letter. I wasn't sure how to handle this delicate situation. Anna was pretty imaginative writing a want ad and all. But to sell into bondage another person's cat—I mean, that is pretty low. I thought of not telling her I didn't send it, then every time the phone rang she'd wonder if it was for her and she'd get pretty frustrated, but I decided that it would be too hard on her already overstrained nerves.

I came home with the letter and immediately confronted her with the evidence. She was surprisingly apologetic. She knew she had done wrong I had to punish her, however, so I banished her to the basement. In time I felt sorry for her and went down to have a purr-to-purr talk with her about her neuroses, frustrations, and other adaptation difficulties since Nerissa had arrived. It did her a world of good, so I doubt she will try to sell Nerissa again.

Love, Dad

From Nerissa to Bruce: *This is my favorite photo. Up here I can see everything. I can keep an eye on Anna, so when I get bored, I can attack her. Also notice I am carefully protecting your speaker. I know you will want this back when you return home, so I don't let them abuse it. As you can see, the light is on. I like the limelight.*

Letters Home

February 3, 1982

Through

March 31, 1982

February 3, 1982

Hello All,

I just got back from seeing <u>Les Aventureurs de l'Arche Perdue</u> (Raiders of the Lost Ark), in French naturally.

Things are going very well. The mail is now flooding in. I get two or three letters a day that were written back in November and December.

I'm quite settled in. I don't eat any more meals at the university because it's too expensive, and eating on the street is a lot more interesting. I've already got my favorite "rice lady." I also found an addiction to replace Bailey's frappes—hot chocolate. They have hot drink tables as part of the street delicacies. They serve hot Ovaltine and Milo, which is Nestle's Quick vitamin fortified to compete with Ovaltine. I have my beverage custom-made, telling them how much sugar, milk and chocolate I want. I've had a lot of fun experimenting with mocha, coffee and cocoa combinations. It's the Coffee Connection in Cambridge sans intellectuals and German Forest cake. I think it's the canned condensed sweet milk with which they make everything that has me hooked.

As I write this letter, I'm munching on another addictive Togo taste treat—cashews. They are freshly roasted by the "nut ladies" and are the largest, sweetest, meatiest nuts I've ever tasted. I also hardly make it through the day without buying a fresh pineapple. How much is this epicurean escapade costing? Bowl of coffee/cocoa: 50-90 francs (15 to 25 cents); quart of cashews: 800 francs ($2.50); and one large, freshly cut pineapple (I eat the whole thing): 200 francs (70 cents).

I got cards from Don and Grandma and Grandpa yesterday, and today I got Dad's letter. I also got Mom's December 14th letter. I think

I've already answered most of the questions you asked. By the way, my dream has stopped, which is a shame because I was starting to have fun with it. Happy Valentine's Day!

Love,
Bruce

February 11, 1982

Hey Folks,

Many letters today! One from my tutor Tom Schwartz with lots of good info for my curriculum next year. And Dad's snowy Christmas card. No fudge yet. Oh, fudge!

Sharyl's letter with the cat article. Thanks, but the American Cultural Center gets *Time*. I was going to send the same article to you, but I knew you'd run across it. I'm hanging the Garfield comics up as a colorful, growing poster on my wall. Television is funny here. There is only one TV station, and TV shows are only on from 7 to 10:30 p.m.—7 to 8 p.m., educational shows; 8 to 10 p.m., movie or sports specials; 10 to 10:30 p.m., news. No commercials except to promote their grain company's drive for self-sufficiency in agriculture. Sharyl, you look great in your pictures.

Great card. I Xeroxed the Nerissa Report and Sharyl's comments to send to Steve. I got a letter from him the other day. He's really having a ball skiing, drinking beer and meeting fräuleins.

Things are really busy these days. I'm definitely over my culture shock. Lots of successful work for DA&A. I think they're impressed. I'm impressed at least. And I know I can count on you to be impressed, even if you aren't.

I've enclosed:
An article on "couth." I read it and recalled many an elbow on the table and noisy eating, pre-Phoenix Club days.

An article describing Kente cloth.

A piece of Kente cloth! When they sew the hand-woven strips together to make broad, resplendently stunning pieces of fabric, the basic technique is just like those yarn belts we made with Popsicle stick looms at the church's Christmas workshop. I have seen these guys make the cloth. It looks like someone playing the organ, with the colorful score revealing itself in wefts and twills instead clefs and trills.

I have also enclosed a chart I found in the American Embassy newsletter "Atupani," which means "talking drums," that briefly outlines the stages and symptoms of culture shock. You can follow my development through the stages, as evidenced by my letters, and see if you think they apply to my experience. They introduce the chart with this description:

Cultural Awareness and Culture Shock

Each of us as Americans and individuals carries a different bundle of values, beliefs, assumptions, attitudes, and concepts of reality with us when we move overseas. This bundle is usually invisible to us because we are immersed in an environment in which most of our friends, associates and colleagues carry a similar cultural baggage. We are rarely required to stop and examine them.

It is only when confronted by others whose cultural values contrast and/or conflict with ours that we have the opportunity to gain insight and self-awareness regarding our own cultural baggage. For most people, this can be a very unsettling experience—a sort of shaking of one's emotional foundations. This challenge to our unexamined assumptions is one of the major causes of cross-cultural stress and shock.

Enjoy!

Love,
Bruce

CULTURE SHOCK STAGES AND SYMPTOMS

	PRE-DEPARTURE	1ST MONTH	2ND MONTH
GENERAL ATTITUDES	ANTICIPATION	EXHILARATION	BEWILDERMENT, DISENCHANTMENT, RESTLESSNESS, IMPATIENCE
SIGNIFICANT EVENTS	Planning, Packing, Processing, Partying.	Red carpet welcome, New office, New colleagues, Temporary or permanent quarters, Exploration of sights and shops, Duty familiarization.	Language study, Housekeeping servants, Full-duty responsibilities, Shipment delayed, Unfamiliar sounds, smells, food manners, language, Cost of living new, Local travel complications.
EMOTIONAL RESPONSES TO EVENTS	Excitement, Enthusiasm, Some trepidation of unknown, Concern about leaving Family, friends, lovers; Familiar environment.	Sense of mission, Tourist enthusiasm.	Qualms, uncertainty, Restless, irritable, Search for security in familiar activities, (homemaking, church, clubs), Some withdrawal, Occasional inclination to relax, Morals, increase alcohol consumption, be loudmouthed.
ATTITUDINAL AND BEHAVIORAL RESPONSES TO EVENTS	Anticipation, Slack-off of interest in current responsibilities.	Outward curiosity about nationals, Avoidance of negative stereotypes, Enthusiasm for colleagues.	Neutral toward environment, Skepticism, uncertainty, Frustration, Question values of people, self, and job.

CULTURE SHOCK STAGES AND SYMPTOMS

	3RD MONTH	4TH – 5TH MONTH	6TH MONTH	24th MONTH
GENERAL ATTITUDES	DISCOURAGE-MENT, IRRITABILITY	GRADUAL RECOVERY	NORMAL	SLACK-OFF PHASE
SIGNIFICANT EVENTS	Cut down or stop language study, Drift to U.S. recreational centers, Uneven job performance.	Resume language study, Acceptable duty performance.	Normal duty performance .	Planning for more travel, packing, new location, schools. Turn over job, Decrease Production.
EMOTIONAL RESPONSE TO EVENTS	Discouragement, bewilderment, Suspicion of servants, Concern for sanitation, (water, food, air) Homesickness.	Interest or resignation.	Equilibrium.	Disinterest in local affairs, Anticipation of next activity.
ATTITUDINAL AND BEHAVIORAL RESPONSE TO EVENTS	Avoid contact with local populace, Withdraw, Become introspective, antagonistic. Fear theft, injury, contamination, Develop antipathy for names, colors, sounds, smells, local manners, Invoke stereotypes.	Constructive attitudes, Accommoda-tion.	Equilibrium.	Occasionally, but not frequently, this is a high production phase.
PHYSICAL RESPONSE TO EVENTS	Minor illness (request sick leave).	Normal health.		

February 16, 1982

Hello Everyone,

I love your letters. Letters are starting to come from other people as well. I got two letters from Fred, including one 12-page tome. The bad weather in Vermont seems to be cutting into the number of his incoming visitors, just as the lack of work cuts into his financial income.

Thanks for the Garfield book. I guess people really know me; Steve sent me the same book for Christmas. I'm also sending Steve extra copies of your fantastic Nerissa reports. He started his last letter to me with a whole page of Nerissa nostalgia. He misses her as much as I do. I sent him my copies of Nerissa Christmas photos, so please make copies of those two shots and send them to me for myself. Also, I don't know whether you've sent our family photos yet (I'm anxiously awaiting my copies), but please make up an extra of the one with me holding Nerissa so I can send it off to Steve.

Dad, your sports reports are great. I share them and the articles on the Celtics with an official at the embassy who is originally from Winchester and is a Celtics fanatic. He has diplomatic privileges, so he can keep abreast of developments, but has a difficult time getting hold of the details.

There are two things that are a priority to send in a future Care package. I'd like my other Stevie Wonder tape, and a new pair of good old Nike Bruins, size 12. Please call DA&A before you get these because I'm going to ask them to try to get a pair for me also if someone from the office is planning a trip to Togo.

Life is going very smoothly. Work is still going strong. And I've discovered three more delicacies:

Cream of Wheat or Farina. Street women serve it out of large calabashes, piping hot. It is the same stuff as our Cream of Wheat, only it is more watery. It is cooked in water flavored slightly by lemon grass, which gives the water a nicely tart quality. They also add freshly home-roasted peanuts. It is great, and I have it for breakfast every day. You should try dry-roasted peanuts with Cream of Wheat.

Tapioca! The original tapioca. Tapioca comes from the African grain marioca, which is used as a starch, mostly for fish dishes. But the Togolese also make tapioca pudding, just like at home, only fresher. They add peanuts to tapioca also.

Coconut-caramel candy. A homemade specialty available in the grand marché.

No stomach problems at all except yesterday, but I deserved it after eating a whole pineapple, which I craved, for lunch.

The letters are starting to come through in about three weeks now, so keep up the writing.

I saw *Superman* at the American Cultural Center. In the film, he says his vital statistics are 6'4", 225 lbs, so I've decided since I've already got the right height, I should shoot for that weight when I start working out again at Harvard. I was 220 at my peak last year.

One of the Peace Corps volunteers here has dubbed me the "Reagan Peace Corps"—a young guy working to help an underdeveloped country by promoting private industry while living there on a subsistence income. I thought that was pretty accurate.

Still NO FUDGE!!

Love you all,
Bruce

February 19, 1982

Dear Mom, Dad, Sharyl, Nerissa, Sparkle, and Anna,

Yesterday I gave a class on the Declaration of Independence for the AIS Junior High. It went really well and was quite exciting. It was a challenge to simplify the complex issues and communicate them to the students. I felt frustrated going outside of the usual, sophisticated avenues of communication that I have gotten used to at Harvard.

I'm putting on a little weight from my high starch diet and lack of basketball at the university for the past few weeks due to exams for the others and now the lights—needed because the sun sets by 6 pm—are broken. I've taken up running with Aaron, my good friend from Nigeria who lives at the satellite with me. That is very refreshing and relaxing.

Enclosed are Kente cloth bookmarks for everyone and a Celtics article for Dad. I have also enclosed my new business card, designed to introduce me as a Togo Information Service researcher for Apter.

An updated food report & new cravings:

I have made peanut brittle!

Steaming hot Ovaltine. For 30 francs (10 cents) at the university I get a baguette with either cheese or jam and a mug of either a ladle of coffee and a ladle of hot milk, or two ladles of hot milk. I get the latte and add tons of my own Ovaltine powder and have a delicious gigantic cup of hot chocolate every morning.

Togolese cookies with their milk, which is not fresh, but made from imported powder, cream, dairy whey, etc. It's no comparison to our West Lynn Creamery's skim. It's kind of like buttermilk. Too rich. The American School serves it cold. The cookies here don't have much butter or shortening, so the milk goes well with them.

I have cookies and milk every day.[17]

I saw a triple feature last night on the Betamax owned by an AIS teacher—*Man With the Golden Gun, The Muppet Movie* and *The Life of Brian*. Tonight, another AIS teacher and I are going to see *Fame*, in French.

The exchange students from the University of California have arrived at Village du Benin. Four females! Their names are Barbara, Jenny, Julie, and Karen. UCal has an exchange program with the Université de Benin, and several students come over every year. Because they all are fluent in French, they will be taking regular university courses; for example, I found out that Julie is studying linguistics and doing research on the native languages of Togo, and Barbara is studying zoology and will be researching African birds. I look forward to spending time with them.

Looking forward to your call!

Love,
Bruce

---

[17] *Bruce's cookies and milk habit preceded Robert Fulghum's insight in* <u>All I Ever Needed To Know I Learned in Kindergarten</u> *that "warm cookies and cold milk are good for you." Sometimes I think that Bruce was on a search in Africa for the ultimate comfort food.*

February 23, 1982

Dear Mom, Dad, Sharyl, Nerissa, Sparkle, and Anna,

Now that I know the ropes and tricks of the place, I'm really settled in, living more comfortably and keeping expenses low.

We will have to keep the upcoming phone call to greetings. I've straightened out the confusion at the switchboard, so call the same way you did before and don't hesitate to ask for George Brown if there is any confusion. I talked to DA&A for about a half hour last week because there was so much going on so quickly.

What are these pressing things, you ask? Well, my average day starts at 7 a.m. when I get up, take a cold shower, shave, dress, and get my breakfast of bread and hot milk, to which I add my Ovaltine in heaping teaspoons. My gardien, a university maintenance man, comes in each morning to empty my wastebasket.

I take my mobylette to the Hôtel de la Paix to see if I have received any telexes. DA&A sends me one usually every to every other day, and I send them out just as often. At 7:30 to 9:30 I run around talking to people, asking questions, researching and making any necessary arrangements or completing tasks they ask of me. From 9:30 to 11:00 I coach the basketball team at AIS. From 11 to 12:30 I'm back to work. 12:30 to 1, I grab lunch at the cafeteria or from my "chicken lady," who has also introduced me to a great maroi (the native fish) dish she makes with haricots (kidney beans).

From 1:00 to 2:30 I get what I have done during the day organized at my dorm room/office. I write any necessary memos, letters, etc. Generally, I recoup for my afternoon foray into "salles d'attente" (waiting rooms) and offices. The things I do for DA&A are:

Picture taking. DA&A needs photos for its publicity and my Canon SureShot is getting a real workout.

Arrangements. I do a lot of advance work—reservations and beforehand meetings with the people the visitors will see, including groundwork research of the field for visiting businessmen, especially tour operators.

Researching articles. I am writing articles on subjects of interest. Some come from DA&A, some are my own initiative. I recently wrote an article on the Medfly research being done in Togo. I will have DA&A get you copies of any of my articles that are published in the American press or DA&A's upcoming publication, the *Togo Journal*. The journal is really my purported raison d'être here. David wants to start putting out a promo magazine on Togo to a list he has made up over the past two years of anyone in America or Canada who ever expressed the slightest interest in Togo. He therefore needs interesting copy as well as support facts and questions answered for articles to be written by our professional staff writer, Beth Bogart. You are on the mailing list.

.   Question/Inquiry answering. This has been 40% of my work. DA&A and the Togo Information Service (TIS) act as a virtual Togolese Embassy public relations charge. In fact, the Togolese
Embassy in Washington sends most of its inquiries from the U.S. public to us to answer. Lately, the questions are coming fast and furious. TIS had tremendous difficulties answering them because of the unreliable action by government contacts lost in a bureaucratic haze over here. Now, if they get a question, I and my mobylette can generally ferret out a complete response within 24 hours and send it to Apter in Washington. Today I spent my morning meeting people at the new record studio and pressing plant in Lomé, touring it, asking questions, and establishing contacts. I guess several American investors are interested in it and want more information.

DA&A public relations. I am DA&A's representative here, so I am constantly calling on people and contacts to relay greetings and news from DA&A.

Hope everyone is well.

Love,
Bruce

February 28, 1982

Dear Mom, Dad, Sharyl, Nerissa, Sparkle, and Anna,

I have come up with three descriptions of myself in my work here. I already told you about the "Reagan Peace Corps Volunteer." I also see myself as half gofer, half guinea pig. Also, half freelance consultant, half indentured servant.

The Togolese and the Americans here don't have such a different attitude toward TV. The two nationalities have entirely different situations, but the general attitude is the same. For the Americans, TV is a luxury and rarity. The only American TV comes from videotapes sent over by friends in the States. An American who has received a video tape will hold a party to show it on his cassette player, and it is a big event. Also, only the best stuff is watched because of the limitation of the number of cassettes we can afford to send. The specialness for the Togolese of TV is much the same. Basically, news and one movie each night. Those two shows are major events of the day and whatever their quality, they are appreciated all the more because of their dearness.

Sharyl, you are not behind or doing poorly. Your PSATs and grades are not far from mine. I think you have what I call the Trip Syndrome, so named for the star basketball player on the AIS team. He is a model case of the disease. The bacterium that inflicts it— giftedness—is not harmful in itself, but only in how the body reacts to it. Trip is an incredibly talented guy, the son of an American Embassy official. He is planning on enrolling in Choate next year. His perception and intelligence are looked to by all the teachers at AIS to pull along the slower ones, who, due to the small size of the school, are inevitably mixed with the smart ones. The teachers tell me their daily frustrations with Trip, who does not contribute and does just the minimum to get by. One teacher explained, "He knows he doesn't have to do much and still do well, so he just does the minimum."

95

I think this syndrome comes from gifted students not being challenged, so they get bored. Active participation ends up taking too much energy in just overcoming boredom. Also, gifted students are not dumb! They are not going to waste valuable energy and mind power on trivial matters and exercises that too often dominate traditional teaching. Those ten points from 80 to 90 have a prohibitively high mental cost. Whereas getting a *B* takes a 10% effort, getting an *A* takes a 90% effort. A dimwitted broker would argue against such an investment.

I have realized this is my own lifestyle. I always shoot for the *B*s in my responsibilities (i.e., things that don't excite me, but I have to do) and I shoot for the *A*s in activities for which I have a natural spark and reservoir of energy, i.e., Africa, SATs, words, sports, and in the future, family. This way I can accomplish the maximum in my life with a minimum of stress.

There aren't many things in which I shoot for *A*s. I have always followed Bacon's and Hobbes's philosophy on the apotheosis of moderation. Any mathematician knows the steep gradient at the very end of the curve, so I shoot for the upper middle in each individual exploit.

You and Trip follow the same naturally expected tendencies of giving the mere minimum when you know it will get you 80% of what you want. The problem comes in what you decide to do with the boon income of energy and resources that you conserved in the classroom. I invested it in numerous, diverse pursuits, some of which I pursued at 80% effort; others I went into 110%. Trip and you don't seem to have chosen those other channels of investment. Trip has basketball, for which he has achieved an A+, but it is obvious from his Atari-preoccupation that there are still countless idle reserves. What is your investment in yourself? In your personality? In your enlightenment? Knowledge? Abilities? Your grades are perfectly acceptable, but what are you doing with your stored-up energies?

I guess psycho-sociologically appropriate is the model of my lifestyle, and possibly Dad's with his generally laid-back style and "let it be" attitude, compared to Mom's always shooting for an *A* and excellence. It is Dad who taught me how to live life. Mom has taught me the pinnacles of success and pleasure in that life. Dad is the sauce, Mom is the spice. In you, Sharyl, I see the laid-back attitude of Dad, but I think you are modeling yourself on a different manifestation of Mom's excellence. I think you care less for credited, spotlight success and prefer subtler preeminence in human relations.

Dad, thanks for your thoughts on marriage. I appreciate the thoughts so warmly and clearly expressed, although they and a million other insights into women and love have already crossed my mind in my preoccupation on this subject, and millions more should continue in the future. There are probably a few things I could teach you about women at this point.

Don't worry. As usual, I am thinking three years ahead of myself, literally. I will in no way nor under any circumstances consider that part of my life (marriage) until this one(study) is finished; however, I may prepare myself for that subsequent stage. I will always appreciate your pensées on this subject to stimulate my own during my years of preparation. However, most important, I'm counting on your coaching when I'm actually out on the court in a real game. Then all the drills of dating and all our "chalk talks" mean nothing and one has to hope I have really absorbed a minute fraction of what I've discovered.

I have always revered the maxim that "education is what's left when you've forgotten everything." My corollary is that "maturity is what's left when you don't have the time or ability to think." As we've seen with many a Shakespearean romance, "love destroys all" and sweeps away all sense of sobriety. That is its thrill and terror. I will need you and other intimate friends to call the time-outs, allow me to catch my breath, and make sure I'm playing my game when it begins.

As for your views on women, I do find them very stereotypical, and I hope and demand that there are many exceptions to this purported career-obsession in successful women. There have to be some sharp, bright, attractive women who could have the world in the palm of their hand, but still realize it's not half as rewarding as holding the hand of someone who is special.

The AIS B'ball team is having a respite to prepare for a series of volleyball games against the French school. Volleyball is not a lawn game here, but a competitive sport. I have been playing it with the Americans for a long time, but our group is starting to get really serious. My sports schedule meshes perfectly and I am not so much getting in good condition as I am really improving my coordination and concentration. Here's my week:

MONDAY: Volleyball against the French and Germans.
TUESDAY: "Football" soccer with the British who work at the BP refinery here and some Togolese. That is a fun sport, and they are tremendous at it. I used to play soccer every Friday with the crew team during the off-season, so it brings back some fond memories.
WEDNESDAY: B'ball with the University of Benin team
THURSDAY: Soccer
FRIDAY: B'ball
SATURDAY: Volleyball with the Americans
SUNDAY: Volleyball and a five-mile run

I've conquered the army ants. They are as fascinating as Lewis Thomas' *Lives of a Cell* makes them out to be, but they are a pain. So now I keep provisions in my room for a sandwich and coffee or hot chocolate whenever I please.

Love,
Bruce

March 6, 1982

Dear Folks,

David Apter is here now to help plan the African Travel Congress coming here at the end of April.

Life is running along so rapidly that I fear I won't find the pieces of time to jot down all that has been going on. Just a food report would take several pages to describe my three times daily gourmet, five-star fetes. Escargots. Coquille St. Jacques (not as good as Mom's, though). Margret canard. Filet mignon. Coconut soup. Croissants and café au lait in bed every morning. The big joke in DA&A now is how I "sleep around." They have me so busy that I sleep in rooms at the Hotel 2 Février and here at the Sarakawa Hotel, depending on where I end up at the end of a very busy day.

The work experience is as varied and spicy as the food. Just working every day with David and Togo's legal counsel, Gil Carter, and international lawyer and Togo's business consultant, Stanley Cleveland, has made me privy to a great wealth of information as well as a firsthand apprenticeship in international business, diplomacy and public relations. I have been to cocktail parties in Lomé with various diplomats from India, Brazil and France. I've become well acquainted with the American ambassador here as well as a slew of American journalists. David has put me in sole charge of a television crew that has come to film a show for cable television and a promotional piece for DA&A. My French is shining. I've become closer friends with many of the ministers—justice, foreign affairs, information, tourism—and I might be meeting the president sometime this week.

In all, I'm in the lap of luxury enjoying a fascinating and unique intensive course in business and diplomacy that could never be engineered in any normal job or training program.

The strokes have been just as great, if not the highlight of these weeks. Everybody is extremely laudatory of my work. The best one came from David. David used to do PR for the State Department, i.e., press releases on events; he wrote the press release that was to be released if John Glenn's space mission were to fail, and he still has many friends there. He was talking to the Director of the African Region, who told David that Washington was getting all sorts of information lately from the Deputy Chief of Mission and Chargé d'affaires in the Ambassador's absence. The State Department official asked the Charge d'Affaires how come he suddenly knew so much of what was going on in Togo, and he told him he got all his information from this Bruce Lynn guy in town. David told the D.C. official that he was going to send the State Department a bill for my services as an unofficial liaison between the U.S. and Togolese governments.

I'm taking a temporary respite from basketball because of my congress activities. The AIS's latest start-up games went very well. The nicest success was the games played when I had to work with the television crew. The crew decided to come along to the game. The teams had been holding practices without me while I was busy with work, and yesterday they played with the help of our Captain Trip. The JVs had their best game ever against the French. I got back at half time of the varsity game, and they were tied at 14-14. Then they tore away, probably under the inducement of the TV cameras.

It's a very nice feeling to get something started and organized so well that it runs itself. The teams will only lose two players through graduation, so I think I've started a basketball tradition at AIS that will continue long after I've gone. Everyone is looking forward to playing the Togolese EZE Club team.[18] Both the JV and varsity teams are 0 for 2 against EZE, but we played poorly both times. Also, EZE has not used girls as we have, but this coming game they will be going coed too. The teams are really improving rapidly, and we are

---

[18] *EZE is a recreational club that has a youth basketball team.*

going to play in the National Stadium—Lome's equivalent of the Boston Garden. I think with all these new factors added up, both AIS teams have a strong shot for a first victory.

Also, the University of Benin basketball team started its season two Saturdays ago against the University of Lagos. I started for UB in my first international athletic competition. That was exciting. I'm sorry I didn't get any pictures, as the teams have very sharp, bright uniforms. Togo really supports its athletes, and all the UB teams are outfitted with flashy new Adidas [sneakers], silk suits, and warm-up suits. The UB colors are purple and yellow. It was quite interesting to see the Nigerian team, who had worse shirts than Ipswich High School's, and each player had to provide his own, mismatching, shorts. UB won by quite a bit; I got two baskets and a slew of rebounds. The schedule is very irregular, so I don't know when we will be playing again.

So long for now,
Bruce

March 15, 1982

Dear Mom, Dad, Sharyl, Nerissa, Sparkle, and Anna,

Hello. Thanks for the great Care package. I'm really looking forward to reading those books, which will hold me for a long time. In the future, if you hitch up with someone coming to Togo, these are the books remaining that I would like: *The Iliad* (it's in my room), *The Distant Mirror* (also in my room) and *Anna Karenina*.

A distinct lull in letters, none in two weeks. Then again, I haven't been writing as much as I have in the past. Life is so busy these days, mostly from the wild life with these California girls.[19] Also, I'm doing a lot of reading. Bible report: Samuel 2. Movie report: *The Blues Brothers* (dubbed in French) and *Deerhunter*.

Of late, I've been confronted by a unique, for me, problem: weight. I've really put on a paunch this past month. My physical activity is just getting rolling again, but is still nothing compared to competitive daily Harvard crew along with my self-initiated weight training and intramurals. This past week I've noticed my flaccidity and the shrinking pants, so I took some appropriate measures.

I will always live by the tenet that, within limits, one cannot eat too much and get fat; one can only be too inactive. But then I've realized that there will come times in my life, such as now, when pressures and commitments take precedence over my athletic ritual and ideal working-out conditions of facilities and schedules. Thus, I am learning how to moderate my intake to balance these pressures. For the most part, I have just finally and sensibly cut down all the excessive quantities of delicious rice and starch I eat here. Occasionally I have even done without a pastry or third serving to trim my midsection. I am looking forward to getting back to

---

[19] *Bruce's inimitable way of exaggerating to mean the opposite, and possibly to push Mom's worry button.*

Harvard's equipment, especially weight lifting. I always feel that my body is in a healthy and attractive condition; however, there is sort of a perverse joy in having let myself go in Africa and observing my and others' reactions.

Glad to hear Nerissa is doing fine. Steve and I are dying to have her back. We'll have a larger suite this year, but we will have to work something out for her in-and-out syndrome. "Arowwnnn" at Sparkle for me.

Keep the Celtics articles coming. There is a whole circle of Celtics fans from America with whom I share them.

Toute a l'heure,

Bye-Bye-Lo,
Bruce

March 17, 1982

Happy Birthday, Mom!

Hello All,

Today has been by far one of the most exciting days of my stay here.

Your phone call was terrific. You all sound great. I did some accounting and found that at the end of May I should have around $1,000 saved up. I am mostly ahead with my work for Apter, and my reading is going very well. I got home and had received Dad's terrific Nerissa Photo Report. I'm sending a copy to Steve. Will you send him the photos? The omnipresent enclosures were terrific.

Today I visited with Barbara, one of the sharp-looking California girls who is becoming a good friend. We laughed for an hour in the sun on how sweet our life is. We'll be going to lunch in a little while for chicken in fresh peanut sauce and homemade yogurt with fresh tropical fruit (mangos and papayas are in season), all for 90 cents.

This afternoon I'm going to read the Bible and one of my history books, then go to the American Cultural Center to read the papers and share the Celtics articles with my friends. The afternoon holds a basketball game against the law school. Tonight, André is having a dinner party. Barbara and I are going to work on our Ewe, and I will read Sartre's *Huit Clos* with my human French dictionaries at my side. Then I may "crash," as I did last night, on Andre's couch.

Hard knock life, eh?? Hardly! Fantastical. Paradisiacal perhaps.

Take care.

Love,
Bruce

March 22, 1982

Dear Mom, Dad, Sharyl, Sparkle, Nerissa, and Anna,

Life is going better than ever. I'm now working on two government committees to make further plans for the African Travel Congress. The work is a fascinating and quite prestigious look into African politics. I'm finishing my article about Togolese ocean fishing and the time I went out with the fishermen.

I'm up to Kings in the Old Testament. I read constantly, day and night. I have a great tan too. Most Saturday nights André, the girls from California, some other friends, and I go out at 11 pm to go dancing and don't get back until 5 a.m.

I occasionally miss some American food even though I'm sated daily with African delicacies. I miss you all, but not as much as before. I miss Harvard, but only its fun parts—social life, parties, intellectual chatting, Nautilus, coffeehouses. I know as soon as I get back, the traumas of social vicissitudes, tests and papers, high costs, sleepless nights, and daily pressures will be more the reality. When I think of that, I realize that I am presently blessed with the most happy and satisfying lifestyle I have ever had or am bound to have for a while. Then again, I felt the same ecstasy my first two years at Harvard. My year here will certainly prompt positive changes in my attitudes and actions when I return, perhaps making my next two years outshine even this paradise.

I am not pressured here. I am constantly learning new things through my extensive and privileged research, through my voracious reading, and through the living classroom of this unique world of Togo. The only thing I bemoan is an occasional shortfall of resources. Athletic facilities are limited, so I am not in as good condition as I prefer. Diet is unique but is limited, which adds to my nostalgia. Transportation on my mobylette is fun but tiring, as it is sometimes too slow. No phones. No mechanization. Little of my favorite entertainment, such as plays and orchestral music.

I have broken the color barrier in Togolese basketball. The Aiglon Club in Togo's National League recruited me to play for them after the University of Benin captain saw how my playing was coming along. I have gotten quite good because of all my playing.

The team members tend to have better skills, such as dribbling and shooting, but I seem to have a better sense in general of the finer points, such as positioning, getting open plays, defensive anticipation, and boxing out. I'll keep you in touch when the season begins.

Love,
Bruce

March 24, 1982

Dear Improving Letter Writers,

I got seven letters today!

Thanks so much for the Hofstadter piece, Dad. Several of my Harvard philosophy professors would sympathize with your lack of appreciation for the profundity of the subject. When I talked to them, they were upset with him for adulterating Gödel's meaning through his simplifying. I applaud Hofstadter's work; however, for all its pungent and punchy expression of much of the magic of the subject, it shot the complete meaning. I also accept his simplifications for the sake of making the fascinating connections between the worlds of religion, philosophy, biology, and mathematics.

Gödel's proposals, as I have stated before to you, seem to undermine the entire notion of man's ever completely "solving" the riddles of the universe. Even though man has jumped to higher and higher levels of cognition, the riddles, by definition, jump ahead even faster. I particularly like his analogy in G.E.B.[20] between self-referential sentences and Zen koans. As soon as you try to "solve" or figure them out, you are stumped. However, if you cease to examine them, they cease to exist. These sentences don't come to life until you read them. But these koans strike the Westerner's nerve from an Occidental point of view.

In sum, the sentences' "unsolveability" or "paradoxicalness" are not their downfall, but rather what makes them interesting, exciting, and worth examining. They are very much like poetry, as R. D. Laing exploits, not only in their ways of playing with the mind, but also in how they do so in a sort of reflection of the awe-inspiring unanswerability of creation, birth, cellular biology, thought itself, and other spectacles of nature.

---

[20] *The book Gödel, Escher, Bach.*

DA&A came through in a big way yesterday. They sent me a big Care package via Air Afrique. Every whim I had ever voiced to them, they satisfied. They had saved every page of the *Washington Post*'s three pages of comics, including Garfield, every day since December 22nd. I read three times a day during the rainy season, but when the sun shines, I make up for it, and my suntan is doing well. DA&A is coming the last week of April and staying for two weeks.

Congratulations, Sharyl, on your play's success. I enjoyed your article on cats. Editorial hint—you write like I used to—very strongly with lively, explicit expression. I have since learned that such spice becomes a sating, amateurish crutch to good writing. Anybody can "express" himself or herself STRONGLY by using super-duper power words and punctuation!! A stylistic rule is to avoid parentheses, quotation marks around single words, exclamation points, and words in all capital letters. They are superficial techniques that create a quick punch but no lasting impact. By emphasizing forceful language and grammar, one tends to sacrifice content. Somewhat ironically, understatement can be more powerful than this style of overstatement.

At Harvard, forcefulness of style is considered tacky. It expresses emotion of the speaker rather than the speaker's using expression to evoke emotion from the reader. The reader should read your astute observations on cats and make the signs, grunts and exclamations himself. When you make them, such as "!*!? scared," you deny the reader the opportunity to feel for himself. Thus, while your composition is exciting, reading it is rather bland. You write, "Isn't that the truth?" but that is something you should leave for the reader to mumble to himself when he reads your perceptive comments. When you say it, you are like someone who dominates a conversation, instead of relying on the silent conversation between a writer and his reader.

My problem on this subject of style is using too many adjectives. I have adopted the rule of only one adjective. If I want to write two adjectives, I find one adjective that embodies the two. It's a tiring and difficult problem; I mean…it's a frustrating problem. Other writers try not to even use adjectives, but choose nouns that are colorful enough to stand on their own.

Great letter Mom. The arms race is a real fascinating issue. It has a life of its own, and I wonder whether the U.S., USSR, or any country really has control over it. The issue has taken on the quality, or lack thereof, of nuclear technology itself with our inability to control it sufficiently. Steve writes me that the issue is really big in Germany. U.S.-USSR power plays are played out in faraway areas like Indochina, Nicaragua, and El Salvador. Perhaps a slight danger exists in the deserts of Nevada. Europe sits under the ominous shadow of a nuclear umbrella.

I pity your weather. Every day I wake up, the sun is shining. The breeze is light and crisp. Each day seems like a different season. Sometimes summer, sometimes spring, and sometimes fall. Each day is the quintessence of that season though. The summer-type days are bright and warm. The spring days are cool in the morning. The fall days are cool in the afternoon. The last thing one is reminded of is winter. A few times in Vermont, Bay Head, and vacations, I have felt the exhilaration of just enjoying the weather, but here I feel it every day, perhaps because it changes ever so subtly. I don't seem to ever get used to its feeling. Every day I walk out I'm struck by how "il fait beau."

Actually, it's the rainy season now. That's a lot of fun and really eerie. Late in a hot afternoon, the temperature will just suddenly drop 15 degrees in 5 minutes. That is quite a refreshing feeling. Then, soon after, a strong wind laden with wisps of water whips by for 15 minutes. Then it starts to sprinkle, and one knows that one has exactly 10 minutes to find cover before it starts raining lions and hyenas. I bruised my arm in several uncovered places from the drops, which seem to be as big as your fist. The lightning is brilliant too because of the heat that has built up. I'm told the rainy season is unusually strong and early this year, just as Harmattan season was.

Getting lots of letters from Harvard buddies. Postcards don't seem to make a difference for speed of delivery. One card I got from you today was the oldest correspondence of the bunch. They are nice decoration for my room, but I fear they are an excuse to get out of writing much. When one writes a letter, one feels obliged to elaborate and expand, thus I prefer them.

Love,
Bruce

March 31, 1982

Dear Sharyl, Dad, Mom, Nerissa, Sparkle, and Anna,

Thanks for the great card, Dad. I like the postcards, but actually I think they take longer. Mom's February 25 card got here just yesterday.

I just finished a lunch of fresh Grand Marché homemade peanut butter sandwiches with freshly baked bread. I started going to a yoga group led by Sri Gian, a good friend of mine who is studying traditional faith healers in Togo for his Ph.D. dissertation. He and his wife have taken over the helm from David and Claudette of the Nurtz Boosters Association and are my best competition, although a legend is already growing in Lomé about my Nurtz playing. Yoga is great for after my sports activities. I'm getting in much better shape. I have even found a weight room in Lomé and am teaching the Togolese some things about weight training.

I recently found out that the gardien who takes care of the property at the university is perhaps not being quite so altruistic in his eagerness to empty my wastepaper basket each week as I thought. And I'm not actually doing him any favors by demurring and offering to do it myself. Today when the gardien's children were hanging around the compound, I noticed that they were playing with some rather peculiar toys—several wheeled contraptions made from a whole host of bits and bobs, all items I had disposed of in my "trash." Shaving can lids, water bottles, paper clips, and pieces of file cards. They all had been salvaged to make an array of gadgets— homemade toys—to entertain the children.

Many of my discarded packaging materials and worn-out possessions are actually relatively rare and particularly useful to working class Togolese. I realize now I had underestimated our simple gardien. I had thought he was being servile and deferential to me, and that I was being noble by offering to take out my own trash, but in actuality I was doing him a disservice. He had been combining a courteous gesture with an angle of strong self-interest—a desire to make something useful and fun for his children.

Bible Report: I'm on Paralipomenon I. Not much progress on studies because I'm devouring my French books as well as French Spiderman comics, because I found out that I'm to be Marc Apter's interpreter when he comes at the end of this month. Hope you like this T-shirt, Sharyl. Bon voyage on your trip.

I'm listening right now to my stereo Walkman and looking out on one of our omnipresent lovely days. I'm anxious to start on my many dreams and goals for next year as well as see everyone, but I wish this Lomé paradise could continue forever.

Love,
Bruce

IV
Family and Friends

The foundations of admirable character lie in a boy's
realistic sense of himself as a human being.
He will never be perfect, and he is what he is because
others have given to him. With such knowledge
comes the possibility of fulfillment, and of character
that will continue to be strengthened by choosing to
do right, and, after failure, to do better the next time.

—*Eli Newberger,* The Men They Will Become

Our home is half a mile from an old Ipswich cemetery containing headstones that date as far back as the 18th century. During one of those classic times in 8th grade when Bruce had to design and construct a "big project" to present to his class, he chose to chronicle all the families in the neighborhood cemetery. He charted every name on every stone, typing the names on little pieces of paper, and then assembled a genealogy of the families resting there on an enormous piece of poster board. It took him weeks to figure out all the connections and relations, all from one original source.

The project proved useful once again when he was searching for college scholarships. He read about a substantial scholarship through the Daughters of the American Revolution (DAR) that required an essay. He chose to write about his self-taught tombstone tutorial in genealogy. He got the scholarship, and Bruce made a point in college not only of reporting back his grades to the DAR — a scholarship requirement — but also of letting Mrs. Hamilton, his contact at the DAR, know how his life was going. He took special pleasure in sending her a picture of one of the unique cemeteries in Togo. The evolution of this 8th grade project into a

113

scholarship and, eventually, into an opportunity to share his Togo experiences years later is characteristic of Bruce's particular way of making connections that endure.

In his last few months in Africa, he exemplified what psychiatrist and author Eli Newberger describes as "emotional literacy." In *The Men They Will Become*, Newberger emphasizes that "boys need to become familiar with feelings and with the vocabulary of feelings, if only to be men of excellent character. This 'emotional literacy' will make them better fathers, and better husbands and professionals." Africa gave Bruce the chance and the time to become familiar with his feelings and express many of them to us for the first time.

Letters Home

April 10, 1982

Through

July 14, 1982

April 10, 1982

Lynns,

It's been quite a while since I've written because I've been busy with work, study and play.

I'm still working on the African Travel Congress. The High Commissioner for Tourism, the president of the Congress, was deposed a couple of days ago and replaced by some guy no one knows. A lot of the politics doesn't concern me, but it has created a lot of confusion. I've also been tied up with needed authorizations for some articles I am writing. In all, the rush of red tape and confusion has just made my job easier as I try to keep myself and DA&A clear of it.

I will be accompanying the next travel writers' trip that will take place directly after the congress during the second week of May. This time DA&A gave me complete control of making the arrangements around a specific set of ideas. I worked with the government's official tour guide, who is a good friend and does a thorough, honest job in planning with me. He will be the guide as he was in December so, like me, he has a vested interest in planning a trip that will work out for the best. DA&A should be leaving to come here the last week in April, so contact or write them to send me anything then.

With the bottlenecks in my job, I have had a boon period for study. I am reading a lot of French to do my best as Marc Apter's official interpreter during the congress, the trip, and for all his Lome business. I've read Jean-Paul Sartre's *Huit Clos* and am now reading Camus' *L'Etrangère*. I've also discovered Spiderman comic books in French, which I devour. Finally, do you remember those Tin Tin hardback, fancy comic books you gave me when I was young to help me learn to read? They have been a part of that disjointed nostalgia of my childhood of Babar and Pooh Bear. I always wondered what became of Tin Tin, and where it came from. In Lomé, I found out that

116

Tin Tin is originally a French book series, and therefore, it is all over the place. So now I am learning my second language the same way I learned my first—comic books, Tin Tin, and words of the day.

I'm also meticulously studying a textbook, the *Economics of Development*, which I got at the American Embassy library. I'm taking reams of notes as well as gathering a collection of Xeroxed articles and dissertations I came across on the subject of development. Considering my study and my experiences, I should be well prepared for the class I plan to take next year on development economics. My first semester schedule should be as follows:

American History Tutorial. My sophomore tutor, Tom Schwartz, has recommended a junior tutor whom he likes and whom several of my tutorial mates have enjoyed this year. His name is Greg Mark; he was a teaching assistant in my American Political History class, and I got to know him because he is also interested in Africa and has worked in Africa. He's in high demand, but Tom finagled in the History Department, and Greg would like to have me there, so I think it should be set. A good junior tutor is key because Junior Tutorial has only three or four students and can be one of the most intensive, rewarding classes of the four years.

Government Junior Tutorial. The Lowell House Government tutor is Michael Schaefer, whose specialty is African political systems. He has traveled extensively in Africa and was a key character in last year's dramatic effort for me to get to Africa. We became very friendly as he shared his ideas, enthusiasm, confidence, experience, slides and contacts to help me. He is also a junior tutor for the Government Department. His tutorial sounded terrific for me, and I wrote him to see if I could work something out. He was quite interested in having someone with my experience to contribute, so he has already pulled strings in the Government Department to give me a reserved spot in his tutorial.

117

These two tutorials will be quite a wealth of fascination, as well as a godsend of instruction. Many students feel fortunate to get one interesting and germane Junior Tutorial, and I will be luxuriating in two top-notch tutors and subjects. I have to mark that down as another direct benefit of my trip to Togo. Given the combination of these pivotal classes and my time in Togo, I'm already gearing toward a thesis topic.

Presently, I'm reading a book called *The-One Party System in the Ivory Coast*. One-party systems are a fascinating phenomenon and generate very intense academic controversy all over the world; however, there have not been any considerable works done on African systems since the early sixties. Also, the foreign minister here, the guy who spoke at Harvard in October, has written several compositions on the one-party system, and he has a lot to say. I'm going to learn as much as I can and then just before I leave, in case I raise touchy questions, I will interview him and several RPT (Rassemblement du Peuple Togolais) officials for some great primary-source information.

In the '60s, all the political analysts went through a lot of justification for these authoritarian systems as suitable for Africa's unique cultural and underdeveloped economic situation; however, since the '60s, all of the successful one-party systems appear to have liberalized and democratized, apparently against the dictates of the strong-rule theory. This liberalization process has been much spoken of in Togo, and I think would make a fascinating senior thesis topic with much potential for success given my resources here and at Harvard.

French Literature. I plan to take a French Literature class to spruce up my French. I'm thinking of taking a course in the Afro-American Department on African literature, conducted in French; however, in Togo I have had a chance to peruse some of Africa's literary offerings and I haven't been too impressed. On the one hand, I think it might be too much Africa in my course load; on the other hand, it would certainly add to my understanding of the vital, down-to-earth cultural framework around which all this theory and history is built.

Developmental Economics. This will be my science course, as I hope to get into an analytically formatted class. There are all sorts of options in this field at Harvard, so I'll scout around during "shopping periods" for something that's enticing. The subject inherently interests me, but I also want to get more business training before I graduate.

That's all for now.

Love,
Bruce

April 12, 1982

Everyone,

I just read Solzhenitsyn's *A Day in the Life of Ivan Ivanovich*, in which he talks a lot about the entirely different levels of appreciation in the prison camp. I could understand what he was talking about, although he was relating a deprivation many levels beyond what I am experiencing. Still, it is provocative to consider how malleable appreciation can be. It can be distended by satiety or concentrated by deprivation. Yet just as much satisfaction can come from Ivan getting an extra bowl of mush as my buying a bottle of apple juice, or the Lynn-Wood-Chadwick crowd going to Seward's[21] for ice cream.

We Americans living here discuss this a great deal, if only to relieve emotions pent up from our appetites. We usually end up laughing. Barbara was all excited today because she bought a tin of tuna fish and a jar of mayonnaise. Jenny went to a birthday party last week where they celebrated by making hamburgers. It's really just a change of availability.

I think when I get home I will feel the same appreciation, only it will be redirected toward homemade foods that I have become so used to here. I know I will crave the African delicacies that I am now sick of; I can't eat fresh pineapple or mangos anymore. Still, in an American context, our yearnings are quite humorously anomalous; for example, the other night we had a veritable smorgasbord, which included a can of soggy Libby's fruit cocktail, Tang and strawberry jam sandwiches, which tasted as good as any gourmet buffet.

Last night I went to see *Casablanca* for the first time at the embassy and bought a Toblerone chocolate bar, another splurge. I will crave Toblerone on any corner of the earth and it is probably cheaper in Togo than in the States. After the movie, a bunch of us

---

[21] *A popular, old-fashioned ice cream parlor in Rutland, Vermont.*

went to get pizza, which was surprisingly good and cheesy. There was even a jukebox, which kept playing American rock, as opposed to this disgusting French disco.

These past two weeks have been Easter vacation, and most of my friends have been traveling, so I've had a lot of time to myself. My tan is getting quite dark because it's been well over 100 degrees every day for the past month. I've also found a weight room, the only one in Togo, at the stadium. It's just like any city weight room in the States, and only a small cadre of guys use it. I've been working out there every day for two weeks and have gotten myself back "en forme." When I'm in the weight room, I feel at home and, as in basketball and other sports, it's an incomparable medium for friendship and sharing.

As you know, my buddies at Harvard rang me up yesterday. That was lots of fun. We are all set with a five-man suite next year that will include Frank Grady, who was one of my roommates freshman year; Mark Scappichio, the president of the Student Council Association when I was the Ipswich High School delegate to Texas; Sid Krieger, a premed from Tennessee, who is the same rough-and-tumble, fun-loving character as Steve; Steve, and me.

Thanks so much for the picture copies of the slides. The Togolese really loved them. Naturally, the one of my mécaniciens is coveted by each of them, so could you send four more copies?

I got a happy note from Valerie Lankford,[22] and I got a downright beautiful letter from Fred. His description of his days and time to himself was as elegant as his handwriting. He just wrote descriptive and heartfelt words of his true love—nature.

---

[22] *A family friend whom we met when she married Menalcus, Ed's classmate at Thomas Starr King School for the Ministry. A therapist, Valerie taught our kids about "strokes"— warm fuzzies and cold pricklies.*

It's been a while since I've gotten letters from you all. I have lots more to say, but things are just happening too fast for paper and pen to keep up. But then, I'll be having lots to say for years to come after this trip.

Love,
Bruce

April 17, 1982

Dear Everyone,

Today is the first lazy, rainy day I've seen since I got here. All my UCal friends—Julie, Jenny, and Barbara—came over to my room this morning for some hot chocolate, music, and reclined chatting. My room has become the center of activity for the Americans at the satellite. With all their traveling in France, they only brought 20 pounds of stuff, most of it essential clothing, so their rooms are very sparse. On the other hand, due to the village's preferential treatment of me (fan, two cushioned chairs, and a double bed), my long stay and the things I brought or acquired (shelves, books, poster, magazines), I have a veritable home. We've been studying all day. Barbara just put Pachelbel on her tape player she brought over, so I thought it would be an ideal time to answer the letters staring at me beside my economics textbook.

It was interesting to hear from you about relationship issues and problems of friends. Relationships have always come so naturally to me and everyone in our family. Of course, work is essential to their success, but either I've grown to accept that without second thought, like doing laundry, or else I've adopted an attitude that a labor of love, or effort of affection, is a fun chore, like washing a car on a summer afternoon, or "doing words" on a Sunday morning.

It is only now as I confront more and more adults on more intimate levels that I realize how blessed and unique are our family's facile relations. My American friends are shocked into hope when they hear me describe my family, especially the love between Mom and Dad. I have always realized that the most valuable gift I received from you has been having you both as role models.

I know so many in the church look to you, Dad, for the same emotional leadership. They are so grateful to have you for one day a week and an occasional get together. I know they all envy Sharyl and me, who are blessed to have had you all our lives. The origin of your role success has always seemed to come from your simple, good life. You took practicing what you preach one step further by preaching and teaching by practicing.

The second most valuable gift you and Mom gave me was freedom. Whenever it was possible and safe, you granted Sharyl and me freedom. This freedom was a tacit way of expressing confidence that meant so much more than words. My friends, both then and now, envy this gift of freedom. I realize now that some people who have never had freedom will never be able to have it. They have been so scripted with lack of confidence in themselves, probably from a lack of confidence in them by their parents, which is further reflective of the parents' insecurity in their role as parents.

What it boils down to is that parents generally pass on to their children their own qualities, be it nature or nurture. Maybe because I've received so few of your physical characteristics,[23] I absorbed that much more of your personal and social attitudes. These thoughts and appreciation come after talking with my American friends, who have been deprived of so much of this emotional wealth.

Work with Apter is fantastic. Everybody is impressed with the job I'm doing. Planning for the congress is going well. I will be taking a two-week travel writers' trip up north in first-class, red-carpet treatment. Also, next week when David arrives, I plan on many fancy meals and lots of fun talking and discussing. Thus, the time ought to fly by until the end of May. With the next three weeks sponging off David's visit, my expenses should be nil, so I can put away another $300. I'm also going to very tactfully and maturely inquire about a bonus for my good, cheap services for college expenses. It shouldn't be too difficult; I think my smooth talking can pull it off. I've already proven that I can find the right job in the real world even under the lowest odds and harshest extremes. This will be my first real-world

---

[23] *Bruce is 6' 4" tall; his Dad is 5' 9".*

negotiation for a raise. Even if it doesn't work out, it will be a great lesson.

The American International School basketball has started up again for two months until the end of school. I'm working out a lot at the weight room and getting back in really strong shape. Drinking a lot of delicious hot chocolate, and eating mostly rice with peanut sauce and homemade yogurt at a little Senegalese spot downtown. The girls and I go there every afternoon.

I have finally discovered good ice cream in Lomé . The place is called "The Milk Bar." The best by far is coconut, which is made with fresh coconut milk! Great way to get hepatitis. If I started to think of all the dangers I impose on myself, I think I'd get sick. But, I haven't had any sickness at all since Christmas, which I think was really "la maladie chez moi." In fact, several people have separately remarked how I always look healthy. They also gag when they see how many vitamins I take: 1 multivitamin, 2 mineral tablets, 6 protein tablets, 1 vitamin C; however, I'm doing things that I thought would have been instant death a few months back. I drink water straight from the wells. I eat anything on the streets. You kind of get a feeling of resignation about preventive measures because there is so much to watch out for. I still take my malaria pills, which is more than I can say for some Americans.

A lot of reading lately. Couple of Steinbeck novels. Lots of French comic books, especially Spiderman. I also saw *Moonraker* with James Bond last week.

Happy Easter and Happy Mother's Day. I missed the sticky buns and rib roast. I've also got a belated birthday and Mother's Day present, which David can bring back.

Love,
Bruce

May 14, 1982

Dear Family,

Enclosed are gifts for you via Apter:

Liberian Batik Dress. Belated birthday gift for Mom. Marie Brown, wife of the director of the Hôtel de la Paix, bought this on my behalf when she visited her home in Monrovia.

Ivory Apple. Belated Mother's Day gift. Please telex me when you receive this package because these things are particularly important, and I will feel better when they are safe in your hands.

AIS T-shirt. A present for Sharyl.

Film. This latest set of slide film ought to keep you busy. I think Murphy (of Murphy's Law fame) must have been a photographer. Included is a roll of 64 ASA film that I accidentally had set on 200 ASA. A friend told me a specialist film-processing lab might be able to do some corrective developing, taking this information into account. Let me know by telex how the slides come out. I stopped writing slide show scripts because events and photos were flashing by too quickly for me to keep track of them, especially with everything else on my mind.

Film, film, film. You asked for it and offered to pay to develop it. If you can figure out a way to send it (maybe via Apter), I could use some more Polaroid and slide film. All this film was taken during the travel writers' trip—the Badou Forest and Cascades, Keran Game Park, the Dzobegan Monastery, Tamberma Mud Castles, etc.

The Last Africans. This book was a Christmas gift to me from George Brown. I thought you'd enjoy reading it.

Lomé. More exciting Togo reading about my new hometown.

Elephant-Hair Bracelet for Dad. The black bracelet is actually made of the hair of an elephant's tail. It is supposed to give the wearer great strength. The Africans have an awesome fascination with elephants and anything attached to or coming from them. During our visit to Keran Game Park we saw an elephant that ended up charging our bus. The bus driver and guide got out of the bus to gather some elephant excrement. They explained that the urine and stools are used in fetishes to make medicines and potions that instill strength. Fortunately for us non-animists, who were not looking forward to driving the next ten hours with a bag of elephant excrement along, the still-belligerent behemoth made a charge at the guide and driver. They were a distance from the bus, continuing to gather, and as the elephant went after them, they split up for fear of their lives. They were able to get away, but that is a whole exciting, incredible story for another day.

Pewter Bracelet for Sharyl. From Upper Volta. Caught my eye.

Tin Tin Books. I wrote you earlier about how I was reading Tin Tin comic books to improve my French. After Sharyl's trip to France, I figure she'll be looking for exciting and fun French reading, so I've enclosed one of my Tin Tin books. It may not have the nostalgia that it has for me, but it is very well written and superb for improving French.

Togolese Magazines, special-issue newspapers, and tourist books. Just some things to give you an idea of my life and the life around me.

Kente Cloth Pillow. Typical.

Bronze Lion from Upper Volta for Sharyl.

"Marriage Chain." A wood carving of two people connected by a chain, all carved out of one piece of wood, that signifies the unity and bonds of marriage.

Enjoy.

Love,
Bruce

May 16, 1982

Dear Lynns,

It's early Sunday evening after a weekend of getting back into my old lifestyle after three weeks of fun and frolicking with DA&A. I've been reading non-stop after being torn away from it for so long, as well as being enticed by the great books you sent along. I have more than enough reading to keep me going, so hold all books until I arrive home.

Ever since I said good-bye on Friday to the last group of DA&A people—Marc Apter, Henri Bersome, and the travel writer trip journalists—I have been preoccupied with home, just as I was during the first three months here. The DA&A trip was a real benchmark that consummated so much of my work. For the next 60 days, I will be doing mostly follow-up work, such as finishing articles I've started, answering questions raised during the trip, covering bases missed by the trip, as well as my usual curiosearching, tidbit sniffing, and running around. Then my last 30 days will be mostly closing out and introducing my replacement.

For the past two nights, I've started having dreams again about being home. They are all generally pleasant, none of the nightmares of before. I no longer have any apprehension at all in Togo, the last vestiges having been swept away by DA&A's constant attention, strokes, and applauding of my work.

I'm looking forward to being home. Many people seem to be departing Lomé at this time and whenever someone else leaves, I think of the day I will be boarding the plane for home. I've already started to do some of the smaller things in preparation for leaving, such as buying gifts. I am not really anxious for anything particular at home, except seeing everyone. Family. Friends. For a long time, I had fantasized about just lying down and listening to my favorite album of Earth, Wind, and Fire, but Sharyl's thoughtfulness has satisfied that. I've listened to the album constantly since I received it. When I gave the album to Sharyl, it was really an all-star "protection present," as I had eyes toward pilfering it for college. I also had a sincere desire to instill in Sharyl a little more varied taste in music outside of the Doors. But now, as I plan to hook up my Walkman to my stereo to play the cassettes, I can use this tape next year at school for continued pleasure. I'm looking forward to sharing my experiences with everyone. We'll have to have a big party where I can show and explain all my slides with the wealth of stories and trivia behind them. Are there any subjects that you feel I have not taken adequate photos of, or ones where my slides did not come out too well?

I'm also looking forward to rediscovering you all when I return. I think we have maintained a real connectedness through our sundry and loving communications, but it would be folly to think that we have any idea where and who each other are after such a year of separation and exciting experiences. Togo. France. Job. Nerissa.

I now understand your anticipation of missing Sharyl when she leaves for college, as I anticipate the departure of my friends to the States. Separation is becoming a growing part of your two lives in relation to Sharyl and me. Hopefully, these instances will inure you to the much greater ones ahead. No children around. Marriage. Moving perhaps some distance away for an extended time. I think at this period in their lives, many couples are swept up by the tide, and separation enters the relationship of the mother and father. I'm sure you will handle the problem quite to the contrary with a deep sigh of relief and only a small sigh of loss. You have always countered the separation with more closeness between yourselves. And again, you will have another context in which to rediscover each other.

I am now up to Judith in my Bible trek. Page 844 of 1,788 pages!

Food is back to good old African street fare. When I was eating lunch today, it hit me that I had gone from the absolute highest class, five-star, Sarakawa Hotel gourmet meal of escargots, shrimp in puff pastry, and two helpings of chocolate mousse, to the world's most basic, cheapest and commonest meal of rice, chicken and bread, all in the course of 24 hours. I also figured out that I could have eaten this basic meal for over 100 days for the cost of one hotel meal.

Not long now till I see you and everyone. I hope the weather there is finally as good as it is here in my endless summer. Give my love to everyone.

Love,
Bruce

May 23, 1982

Mom, Dad, Sharyl, Nerissa, Anna and Sparkle,

I just finished listening to your tape with my two favorite "wives," Jenny and Julie. Barbara has turned out to be another example of a non-responsible drifter, but Jenny and Julie are great. They come over to my comparatively presidential suite, where we can make bottomless cups of hot chocolate while Jenny works on her Ewe word lists for linguistics, Julie writes her research paper on Togo's public school system, and I read my economic development book, write memos, plow through the Bible and other sundry books.

Because the three of us go out all the time together, being with Julie and Jenny is the closest thing I have to dating. Thursday was Ascension Day, which was a national holiday, so Wednesday night we went to see *Force Ten From Navaronne* in French. Then, last night we saw *Song of the South* at the American Cultural Center, and tonight, we are going to see *9 to 5* there. You don't have to worry about my bringing any of them home because they are really half maternal, half sororal friends.

Bible Report: Job. Page 925 out of 1,788. Job has redeemed the Bible for me, although the books previous to Job fascinated me as a historical and cultural study. Their religious implications were depressing and unenlightened, to say the least; however, I would exclude Genesis and Exodus from this categorization. God is a vengeful, arbitrary, and jealous being.

Job has made amends for all that. The words are Shakespearean in eloquence and imagery. The comparisons between Job's introspection and Hamlet's are endless. Job asks some real tough and demanding questions, which basically set the scene for Jesus' arrival. Job is the only thematic conflict in the Bible thus far, but it is a conflict par excellence. He demands passionately and articulately the perplexing questions of all time. Is there justice in life? Can man ever discover all the mysteries of science? Even, What is the meaning of life? Some of his musings remind me of Zen koans.

The book I am reading now on development economics, not surprisingly, has prompted my basic interpretation. Its essential thesis is that the real key to development is a thriving group of entrepreneurs in a country or society. These entrepreneurs need certain iconoclastic qualities from which to be successful, one of the most important and radical of which is the desire to take risks. In the complex, anti-traditional notion of risk-taking are ideas such as accepting that things may not always go right at first, but that one must persevere for a long- run return on investment. In this idea, many complex notions of statistical analysis and probability are embodied.

It is this ethic of patient endurance through injustice that is established by the Book of Job. The rule is one of an arbitrary hand of nature and that chance is blind to wealth or goodness. In a modern economy, failure as well as success is allotted essentially according to the qualities of each economic man, but in the end, irrationality plays just as important a role. Despite Job's demise, he knows and remains confident of the value of his life, just as an entrepreneur who has tried and failed is much more important to society than someone who does not try at all. Job's lesson flies in the face of the tit-for-tat ethic embodied in the histories of Israel, wherein three hins of wine and an epha of wheat equal forgiveness for playing cards on Sunday, and one golden calf idol instantly equates with death.

I think the irrationality and injustice of nature is <u>the</u> basic religious question. Zen Buddhism answers it by accepting it and transcending it. Some of Job's retorts sounded like Zen koans. Jesus answers it with the promise of heaven as the ultimate reward for all injustice suffered. This subject drives science forward into metaphysical studies, which only find more irrational questions and problems.

I think the Bible has this thread of God's irrationality throughout in His sweeping genocides and plagues, but the early Judaic scholars are constantly trying to attribute the source of God's irrationality to some secularly causative and rational source. Not until Job appears, who is supposedly the quintessence of innocence, is the idea of true injustice, i.e., punishment without cause or meaning, developed. Even then, his friends meet Job's inspired questions and cries with the traditional response—he just must have done something along the way to get God's goat.

Job is the first of the books of wisdom. I am anxious to read the others to see if they expand these questions or start to take a stab at the answers. I suspect real satisfactory religious answers are not provided in the Old Testament, creating a call for the books of the prophets to promise the answers and eventually the Gospel, which, in my opinion, finally solves the religious questions and conflicts ignited by Job.

Today is a rainy Sunday, just perfect for such religious musings. Jenny and Julie are eating a breakfast of Ivory Coast hot chocolate, French bread, and French cheese. I am listening to Pachelbel on my Walkman, writing this letter. I'll be speaking to you soon.

Love,
Bruce

May 27, 1982 (78 days till homecoming)

Lynns,

Your package came yesterday via Air Afrique at the most opportune time. Despite your rush, the package did not reach D.C. in time for David's departure; however, the Air Afrique Director was in town, the one who set me up in first class on my trip here, and he said he would courier it to me—sans charge, san formalities. I received it Wednesday. I woke up that day to look out on gray drizzle with a full-fledged cold. Being the dedicated worker I am, and given the work I had to do that day, I trotted through the mist on my mobylette. I got a lot done, but the highlight of the day was receiving your package.

Congratulations, Dad! It was very exciting to hear on tape the surprise party for your 25 years in the ministry and 20 at the Northshore Church. The clippings were great. My fellow Celtics fan went on vacation in the States a week ago. I know it was intended to correspond with the NBA playoffs. When I went to see him this past week, his secretary told me he was staying another week, which I took to mean the Celtics were doing well, and he wanted to be on hand for a repeat championship.

I'm back to my old form in weight lifting. I bring my cassettes and borrow a tape recorder, which the guys at the gym really enjoy. I've also become good friends with a Ghanaian who is about my strength and works out regularly like I do. It makes all the difference in the world to have a partner for weight lifting. My basketball game is in top form too.

In your last letter you mentioned the interest of some people in the cemeteries in Togo. I just sent a letter to the DAR scholarship chairman, Mrs. Hamilton, with a Polaroid of me in front of one, and I talked about the cemeteries here and how they say so much about

135

people and history in their distinctively expressive manner. I also sent her a Togo-American flag pin.

Cortisone cream is extremely valuable during rainy season. The mosquitoes are as thick as the rain. A lot of friends have malaria. Two of the UCal students—Barbara and Karen—have hepatitis but are doing all right, just a little worn down.

Congratulations, Sharyl, on your Student Council presidency. Yes, I have gained weight. I lost it during the three weeks of three full, rich meals during David's visit. Now I'm eating less, exercising more, but still putting some back on. I'm not worried any more about it after losing it so quickly on a Western diet. I'm sure I'll be my old self when I get back to Bailey's frappes and cheeseburgers and get off the high-oil, high-carb, low-protein African fare.

Right now, there is an incessant flapping around my window. One hundred giant termites, six inches long, are flying against my window, attracted by the light. When you see the size and quantity of these African termites, you no longer are astounded by their giant earthen-sawdust homes. When I first heard them as the sun was going down, I thought they were birds outside my window, which now looks like a window of a beehive, only with a swarm of giant African termites flapping all over it. It feels almost like a Hitchcock movie.

I'm doing a lot of reading these days. I'm into the Psalms, which are kind of nice, but slow. Your books are great. Also, a lot of follow-up work on the big trip—questions unanswered, story ideas raised. I've done some research on the "living architecture" idea. There's really a lot to it. I'll fill you in when I get the whole scoop.

Looking forward to your call on Tuesday.

Love,
Bruce

May 30, 1982

Hello,

The French display the inefficiency, pretentiousness, and mismanagement common to their unofficial policy of direct rule in the management of the 2 Février Hotel. Three instances point to a lack of designating responsibility and confidence in lower and middle level African managers.

For example, David went up to the main desk at the 2 Février for information on arrangements for the 1982 African Travel Congress, which would fill the high-rise hotel with hundreds of international delegates for the first time in its existence. The Togolese had been making arrangements with a special government committee for many months to coordinate and inform all concerned parties and sectors in Togo's hotel and tourism industry. Yet the day before the arrival of the delegates, the entire floor staff of Africans knew nothing of what was about to take place in 14 hours. David asked to see the assistant director, a French expatriate, asked him what was going on and why the reception people weren't able to answer his question concerning his room. He responded, "Oh, don't bother them. They don't know anything."

Twice I have gone to the 2 Février for information and permission when the two French directors were out. I was referred to the Togolese floor manager, who was responsible in their absence. Both times, his only action was to tell me that I had to come back to talk to them. Essentially, he was given no decision-making powers; he just tended bar until the directors got back.

In both instances, this attitude of not delegating authority results in deleterious effects. The first effect is inefficiency for the clients. The clients—the Americans and me in this case—have to waste time trying to get in touch with a very limited number of responsible persons. Their authoritarian control increases their responsibilities and thus their inaccessibility. This starts an increasing cycle of difficulty, as their limited time availability means even more waiting time for a client to reach them. David aptly remarked, "200 Americans won't stand for such a runaround. It will be chaos."

The next effect is the inefficiency for the office. The very busy administrators are bothered by simple questions and decisions that could easily have been taken care of or answered by subordinates. Usually the administrators end up simply re-referring the matter to the subordinates, but only after the top has been touched can the subordinates perform their duties.

The third effect is the creation of dependency on the administrators, which has already been shown to result in progressively worsening inefficiency as administrators become more and more tied up. Furthermore, dependency eliminates the possibility of lower and middle, native-born managers assuming higher positions. This has many harmful, indirect effects of perpetuating costly expatriate presence, discouraging advancement and managerial initiative and improvement, and uncomfortable, racially oriented positions of status.

This authoritarian control is an obvious model of the French African head of state, the most notable being Houphouet-Boingy Eyadema and an aspect of Gil Carter's model of central-control inefficiency.

Love,
Bruce

May 31, 1982

Hello Family,

I just thought I would write a letter to bring you up to date with my life, and so I can kind of refresh my mind about what we should talk about when you call tomorrow.

This rainy season has not only brought gigantic corn stalks everywhere, but a whole host of plagues. I've had a nasty cold for over a week, which has really inhibited my activity. The weather is now constantly cloudy and drizzly, meaning very little is possible on my mobylette. However, I've been reading 100 pages a day. I've also done a lot of writing, even though I haven't received any letters since your postcard broadside and your DA&A package. I just got a long letter today from Steve, explaining that he hasn't written because he's been touring Eastern Europe for two full months. It sounds like an incredible trip. Now he's back at school in Munich until the beginning of August.

Colds and chills aren't the only thing this blasted rain brings. The mosquitoes are absolutely swarming, and it's an endless struggle, which I always lose. For the first time in my life I like, or at least can tolerate, spiders, even in my clothes closet. I still kill the hairy, large ones because I'm convinced that they're man eating. But the other smaller ones that I would normally detest at home, I let live peacefully. The corners of my room look a little like an old haunted house, with my tolerance of the cobweb homes increased by seeing their hold on forlorn mosquitoes.

I've created a sort of *Charlotte's Web* rapport with one enterprising spider who has set up roost in my clothes closet and nabs the many mosquitoes that are attracted by the scent on my clothes. Every time I get dressed in the morning, around three bugs fly out of my shirts. Now, only an occasional one escapes the clutches of my hit-spider.

The other problem this rain has brought me is fungus. The moisture in the area, combined with the heat of the skin, incubates the spores. Some Africans have it so bad that they look as though they have leprosy. It doesn't itch, but it is kind of like eczema in that it leaves white splotches and eats away at the skin. The Peace Corps doctor gave me some Selsun formula, which has all but wiped it out.

Showers do no good. As soon as I get out, sweat and smell start up again. Drying clothes is a matter of luck in hitting a patch of sunlight, and I have to be careful of my clothes mildewing. Also, all my cassettes are getting gummed up from the moisture.

Life is not all that bad; it's just that I've got a real stink against this rainy season. Julie and I have subsequently spent a lot of time inside, just reading. Yesterday I started to lament how boring and unexciting life was. She got me good as she went on humorously pointing out that here I was, in the middle of Africa, I was charged by an elephant a week ago, attacked by swarms of giant termites a night ago, meeting exotic people, eating exotic food, traveling first class to jungle cascades and traditional architecture castles, drinking with ministers and ambassadors and international businessmen, riding around on a mobylette discovering the native life... I'm bored?!?

It reminded me of my comments to Don just before I left, that my trip here might be unmatched in excitement for the rest of my life, and Mom's concerns that America will seem so routine after the eccentricities of West Africa. But it seems Africa has already become routine. Either that or adventure has become my life routine, and going back to peaceful, relaxing activities becomes the spice of life.

Talk to you tomorrow (my tomorrow).

Love,
Bruce

June 8, 1982

Dear Family,

Dad, I love your descriptions of the day, but please include the date in your letter so I can judge how the mails are running.

I've enclosed the latest edition of the *Post-Game Gazette*. It was a very thrilling game. It was also a great experience coaching. All season, come hell or high scorers, I arranged things so that just about all the players played equal times, taking into consideration practice attitudes. We were playing our last game against EZE, and our last chance to beat them, when I started putting in some players from the bench. AIS was an entirely different team. The starters were simply playing leagues better than the next platoon, check out the 2nd quarter scoring. So for the rest of the game, I let the standouts play. I rationalized it by the fact that these top players had put their heart into the team all season and come to the Saturday practices, and this game was for them to show their best for AIS. Further, as a team, the bench should be rooting for these players, on whom victory depends, in a team spirit rather than griping individualistically about how much playing they did.

It really shook the school the next day as the players, spoiled by egalitarianism, quibbled in classrooms. Teachers seized the lure of this sports analogy by applying the situation to attitudes and principles in the classroom and life. Several teachers talked to me afterward, telling me how much the kids had learned from the game.

Tomorrow we play the French school in our final match against them. It will be the JVs' last chance to win a game. Next week the varsity team will be playing against a sort of pick-up team of guys who always come to scrimmage with us on Saturday mornings. Everybody in the Quartier comes to watch the AIS games, and this Quartier team will have the thrill of its lifetime playing against us for real, with cheerleaders, spectators, and the whole scene. The guys are really much older than we are, but they don't play ball much, so they're not that good. By then AIS should be in top form for a fun final bout.

After the last match, I'll give out awards and recognitions during promotion exercises. The school offered me the job as P.E.[physical education] teacher next year and begged me to stay. The salary would have been twice what I make with Apter ($200/week). Apter has also asked me repeatedly to stay another year. What with a small raise I could negotiate, plus working P.E., I'd be overworked but living pretty well. But life must go on...

Your letters have been coming virtually every day. I don't know what will happen now with the "Celtics Evo," as the Togolese say, which roughly means "go Celtics, or Celtics great!" I'm just fortunate the NBA [National Basketball Association] season extends so long. I got a kick out of Dad's special effort to send the Celtics Care Packets in chronological order. He obviously has not spent much time in Africa. I think the censors read that, saved your letters, and delivered them in anything but a reasonable sequence. Exempla gratia, I got your letter from March 17 on June 3, then your letter from May 15 on June 4. At least those two letters were in chronological order.

Nerissa has also turned out to be the best catalyst for your writing. I'm afraid to take her in September for fear of suppressing Dad's creative writing. What will he do on a tired-from-tennis-and-yard-work early Saturday morning? I also loved your sermon on alcoholism. You might try getting it published some December. It's quality work, and the subject should jibe well as a human interest, humanitarian piece for a periodical. The length and style are perfect for a national, monthly, middle-class, dentist-table type magazine, not to mention some larger papers.

The letters have been especially appreciated recently as I have been a little dispirited. My cold has passed, but there have been lots of aggravations and disappointments of little importance; at their worst, kind of like African mosquitoes. You can't feel the bite, so even while you have no chance of catching them red snozzled, you can't even get the vengeful pleasure of destroying them.

Most of my friends will have left town by the end of June. I mean, all. A lot has been happening this month and a lot more is scheduled. July will be a very interesting, slower-paced final quarter, I think.

In the Bible, I'm on Proverbs. Good book. No kidding. Lots of fun, witty and wise maxims, and less of "The Lord is my rock, let Him be praised..."

I loved your letter, Sharyl. You are the opposite of me when it comes to French. I can hammer or stammer out just about anything with decent pronunciation and moderate grammar; however, I have a real problem understanding French when I listen to it. Three romances in two weeks! I haven't had that many all year. Something must have happened to you when you got your braces off.

Happy Father's Day, Dad, if my timing is correct. Lots of basketball playing these days. I've gotten quite good. I can even, finally, dunk the ball for the first time in my life.

Cuddle Nerissa for me. Whine hello to Sparkle. And keep an eye on Anna.

Love,
Bruce

June 12, 1982

Dear Family,

Here is my latest write-up of the *Post-Game Gazette*. It describes the Celtic-esque excitement of our double overtime victory over the Quartier "Blues." We play them Wednesday for the final game of the season.

The team virtually runs itself now. They even write their own *Gazette* when I'm not there. One of the 8th grade girls, Claudia, wrote a recent *Gazette* in which she described an official game they pulled together after a heavy rainstorm when everybody, or almost everybody, thought the game was canceled. She wrote, "A lot of players, especially of our team, didn't come because the game had actually been canceled, but I'm glad that we played and beat the EZE Club! One bad thing was that the referee called many fouls on us, most of which weren't true! I tried several times to shoot a basket but I always missed. I think our team cooperated much better than ever before. We passed a lot, for example." You can see, Claudia is learning to express her feelings for the team as well as her disappointments.

Coaching the team has been a great source of enjoyment and satisfaction for me. When I'm late for practice, they run practice themselves. I have built a virtual C.E.G. (the French equivalent of junior high) basketball league with four teams—the French, EZE, AIS and Quartier—and a ten-game season. The AIS is hiring a new P.E. teacher next year and the major qualification is that he know how to teach basketball! On Friday, I'm doing the sports award presentation for the team.

In keeping with all the confusion inherent in West African mail delivery, I got Mom's April 5 school-committee-time-passing letter yesterday. The day before, I got a birthday card from Uncle Alan and Aunt Judy and family. That made seven straight business days of letters. I'm working on a streak. That already breaks the record, but I'm going for the magic number of 18.

I was sorry to hear that Mom had a bit of a confrontation with Marie[24] at the school committee meeting, although I would have suspected that type of behavior and attitude, if not to that extreme a degree. Simply, Marie expects too much from people, including herself.

It has hurt Joan in ways that will affect her and their relationship for the rest of their lives. Her expectations affect me in that I, to tell the truth, avoid contact with her for apprehension of some reprimand of me or one of my friends. One always has to be on the defensive with someone with high expectations, and it is not a comfortable feeling.

When I had conversations with Marie, if an old friend's name came up, she would not say, "I wonder what's happened to him. It's been a long time since I've heard from him. I hope he's doing well. He's probably very busy." Instead, she would reprove, "Well, he obviously doesn't care enough about me to stay in contact. Why should I care about him?"

She's very giving in ways that are easy for herself: cooking, visiting, working. But she expects a quid pro quo return in a way that she would like, not necessarily considering how capable the person is of returning in that manner.

As with many screwed-up things, we turn to cherished benchmarks for some sort of scale to the problem. I think of Fred and Don in comparison to Marie. If we go a year without talking to them, no one pouts or gets angry. We just say, "It's good to hear from you." They are friends who are always there and will always be there even

---

[24] *Marie is the mother of one of Bruce's closest high school friends, Joan. (I have changed both names to maintain anonymity.)*

if circumstances keep us apart for any period of time. Marie is a conditional friend, one only if you buy into her self-centered exchange of what she considers friendship. I wish it were otherwise.

Love,
Bruce

June 18, 1982

Hello Mom, Dad and Sharyl,

Only 56 days until we meet in Paris. If things keep going the way they are, I'm going to have a mighty fine month, with time to reflect on my experiences here.

Today has been such a hectic day I don't know where to begin.

The bad news first. Rain! I have never seen so much rain. It comes down constantly. The only variation in weather is between drizzle and downpour. A good day is determined by how little the mobylette passes out because of the moisture and cold.

Everything is always wet. All the roads are washed out—the Togolese equivalent of Route I-495 being under four feet of water. You just kind of want to sit inside. Even that is uncomfortable. The air is muggy inside and out. Everyone has colds. I'm generally miserable to match the weather despite all the things that are actually going well.

Not finished yet! The Lynns in Ipswich have "Mosquito Alert"; I have "Mosquito Safari"—twice a day. Once before I go to bed. They roost in the closets. Then again in the morning when I find the ones resourceful enough to escape my grasp the prior evening, now so bloated with blood they can barely fly. I've never seen mosquitoes that fill themselves with so much blood. It's kind of fun revenge because they really can hardly move, so they just sort of hop around on the floor. The only problem is that after my tormentingly slow chase and the finish, the blood spurts everywhere. My yellow wall is now red polka dots. I don't wash the wall because they are like notches in a gun butt for me.

I cannot wait for dryness. This really is a land of extremes. I remember how equally cursed the dry Harmattan was. Thin dust

147

everywhere. Chapped skin. However, I prefer that to this. This moisture makes me feel like I'm constantly in wet diapers.

The good news. Today we had the Promotion Exercises at AIS. I've included the *Post-Season Special Edition Gazette* I gave out after the ceremony. My presentation of awards was the big highlight. I also got countless strokes and warm fuzzies. It was nice seeing my work mean so much to the lives of each of them and to build them up at each award, making each recipient feel proud and special in front of the school, their parents, and their teachers.

Yesterday, Trip's father (Trip is the AIS basketball star) invited me over to watch the NCAA [National Collegiate Athletic Association] playoffs a friend had videotaped and sent over. It was quite a shock to see real basketball and a window into American society through the intermittent commercials, although admittedly a basement window. There were so many little things that have altered cars—new brands, gimmicks, and styles. I spent the whole time saying, "Oh yeah!" to myself as I saw things that I had been so long without and had simply forgotten about.

That's all for now. I'm looking forward to tomorrow's call. With some things straightened out, this is an opportunity for a fabulous trip to Europe.

Love,
Bruce

July 1, 1982

Dear Family,

43 days to Paris!

Well, my wives have all left me. Jenny and Julie got a ride to Upper Volta, where they are taking a discount flight to Paris, a bus to London, visiting some friends and then heading back to the big USA.

Congratulations on your hospice magazine, Mom. Congratulations again on your sermon, Dad. Congratulations on the Student Council, Sharyl. I loved the family Nerissa exposé.

This week, this summer's batch of Crossroads Africa people arrived in Lomé. Remember Crossroads? It's kind of eerie to realize that I could have been a part of it. We have hit it off very well very quickly. They are leaving Monday for their project in the northern part of Togo. They are great people and the program is fascinating, but it is just amazing how many leagues ahead of the program my experience has been. Seeing their experiences as an option for where my life here might have gone, gives me perspective on just how miraculously fortunate I have been.

Mom, I've learned how to make the one food I have every single day—rice with peanut butter sauce. I'll teach you how to make it when I get home, along with my other staple—Senegalese yogurt.

I'm writing all my friends in France to alert them of our visit. Patrick from PSK club, Jean, last summer's roommate, and good old Roland.[25]

The rain has stopped even though most of the roads are ruined and bands of outlaw mosquitoes roam the streets late at night.

---

[25] *Bruce's high school exchange student from Paris.*

I've caught up on my DA&A work after a big push this past weekend. Jeanne Kirkpatrick, U.S. Ambassador to the UN, visited Togo with a delegation of women. Today I met her and interviewed Mrs. Dole, wife of Robert Dole; Marylyn Lewis, wife of the Secretary of Transportation; Nancy Reynolds, friend of Reagan's and Pennsylvania Representative; and Ursula Meese, wife of Edwin Meese. During their festivities, I chummed around with "my bosses," who were entertaining them—the Minister of Foreign Affairs and the Minister of Justice, who is the person who interviewed me in New York for this job. It's been pretty exciting—Secret Service, Air Force jet, and all sorts of impressive things.

Now things are slower and the way I like it. Now I can get some more reading and writing done. I'm on Jeremiah in the Bible, page 1,360 of 1,788. Basketball's started up again now that the rainy season seems to have passed.

I've enclosed several photos, one of which shows the goats grazing on the university lawn. Notice the mynah birds on their backs; they eat the fleas and bugs that the goats stir up as they walk through the tall grass. In one of the others, you can see the cornfield fetishes, which are positioned throughout the cornfields to cast a hex on any thieves. Believe me, these things keep the thieves away out of sheer fear!

A tantôt! Brush up on your French. See you in six weeks, five by the time you get this letter.

Love,
Bruce

July 10, 1982

Dear Lynns,

I've just finished the busiest, most tiring week of my stay, and yet it yielded all sorts of success. DA&A work. Moving. Closing out some things. Getting my bags on the way home. So I just thought I'd start off this Saturday morning by skipping basketball practice with the Aiglons, even though there is a summer tournament in two weeks, and write you all a letter. I got an old May 5 letter from Mom this week, written on a lazy afternoon, Dad's paterno-ministerial "bull" (pun intended), and Mom's June 19 letter.

Dad's commentary on the Bible was superb. Thanks. You mention, "You can find just about whatever you want in the Bible." It is that assertion that prompted me to read the Bible. I knew that one could, and many would, take the Bible's contents for different and divergent purposes. Most often when one would do this, it would be in the form of a quote. In the Bible, as in life, many and even most things taken out of context lose their entire meaning. I wanted to read the Bible to find out what the Bible had to say about life, and not just what Isaiah had to say about nuclear disarmament.

Too much use of the Bible is deductive, that is to say, people explaining meaning from small portions. I wanted to find the Bible's inductive messages. Those small ones you pick out of the mass of conflicts, repetitions, and words. Deduction is nearly equivalent to illogic in mathematical reasoning, and yet induction is one of the most elementary and valid methods therein. Yet most people use the former in the form of isolated but broadly interpreted quotations and, as you mention, few people read the entirety and seek out the smaller, more germane, messages.

When one mentions the dullness of the Old Testament, one thinks of all of the begats. But the real difficulty with reading the OT is the use of the ancient literary device of repetition. Phrases and

151

ideas are used and reused literally hundreds of times with slight variations. For a church's yearlong liturgy, the variation is enough to add just a little spice and twist each Sunday, while preserving the basic message. However, in reading it as literature, the variations are too minor to give the repeated messages any literary zest. And yet one cannot even skip over the repetitions, as one could the begats, because in those slight variations lie the very distinctive elements and perspectives that reflect the particular book or author as a whole.

Now that I am at the end of the OT, this difficulty is the most intense, because for all literary purposes, I have read all that the Bible has to say. Yet I am in one of the most influential and important sections, the Books of the Prophets, as they interpret the past books in terms of the coming Messiah. The exact same messages have entirely different meanings. Even discounting these slight variations, much repetition is sheer unaltered, slow-moving repetition for literary and exhortative devices. Yet even these cannot be skipped over, for the extent of their repetition gives us clues as to how valued, needed or important were the sentiments so expressed. There is a big difference between something repeated 200 times and 100 times. And when something is stated in one isolated example, one should really question its validity or priority.

I've talked here about "how" I have read the Old Testament. I have already read the Good Book for Modern Times all the way through, but the OT and the NT are distinct and different works in meaning, effect, and character. In my last letter on the OT, I tossed out some reflections I had on it. My recent thoughts are really more detailed expansions of the same ideas. I see in the OT an expression of mankind's frustration about problems. English classes teach that there are three basic thematic conflicts: man vs. nature, man vs. man, and man vs. himself. And yet while the OT involves all three of these, it delves not just into the various conflicts, but also into the issue of conflict per se. Why is there conflict in the world? Why is there injustice, really a close synonym for conflict as the OT uses it? Why does man fight against himself, nature and others? The answers to these and other pertinent questions vary throughout the OT, and are as different as night and day in the NT and the OT.

It's a sunny Saturday, and I'm going to go to the American Cultural Center to do some words and read the newspapers to find out what happened two weeks ago. Do you realize that I have been doing words for five years now? What are words like after five years? Oubliette, unshriven, seneschal, décemvir, attainder, kabuki, antinomianism. Also, about one third of my "words" these days are names and events that are referred to. I may know something about them, but I look them up in the encyclopedia for the full rundown, such as Silesian, Lycurgus, and Albigensian.

Take care, everyone. See you in four and a half weeks, less time when you receive this. Sharyl, don't worry about missing my stories. You can visit me in Cambridge and hear them when I tell all my friends. Good talking to you yesterday.

Love,
Bruce

July 12, 1982

Dear Nerissa and Nerissa-Lovers and Anna,

The enclosures in your recent letters were great! I opened the letters while my mécanicien was fixing the brakes on my mobylette. I gave each of the mécaniciens a Garfield sticker as a cadeau; they had shown an interest in the newspaper clippings of Garfield comic strips you have been sending me. It was also good to hear about all of the exciting and successful preoccupations and occupations in your lives.

Your other neodiluvial tales[26] reached a sympathetic ear. The rain here has subsided, but it still rains every day. Every single road is a mess. The sand base of the paved road just washes away, and the pavement collapses. Then, in other areas, when the water dries up, it deposits all the sand that was washed out from under the aforementioned road on top of the other roads. So all the roads are filled with either potholes or piles of sand.

I'm finishing up a lot of reading and doing things I like to do. I started making a list of all the books I've read while in Togo, some of which will be useful for the next school year. Thought you'd be interested: *Coups and Military Rule in Africa*, Samuel Calo; *The Guns of August*, Barbara Tuchman; *The Last Africans*, Gert Chesi; *The Castle*, Franz Kafka; *Poetry with Pleasure*, Anthology; *Six Centuries of Great Poetry*, Selections; *The Humor of JFK*, Booton Hendon; *The Proud Tower*, Barbara Tuchman; *Catch 22*, Joseph Heller; *The American Political Tradition*, Richard Hofstadter; *The Lives of a Cell*, Lewis Thomas; *Huit Clos*, Jean-Paul Sartre; *The Odyssey*, Homer; *One Day in The Life of Ivan Ivanovich*, Alexander Solzhenitsyn; *The Pearl*, John Steinbeck; *The History of West Africa vol. 2*, J. FiAde Ajay & Michael Crowder; *The Red Pony*, John Steinbeck; *L'Etangère*, Albert Camus; *The Zimmerman Telegram*, Barbara Tuchman; *Stillwell and the American*

---

[26] *We had written to Bruce about the failure of our sump pump, and the subsequent and significant flooding of our basement.*

Experience in China, Barbara Tuchman; *The Economics of Development*, Everett F. Hagen; *The Best American Humorous Short Stories*, anthology; *West Africa Under Colonial Rule*, Michael Crowder; and, of course, the Bible.

I seem to be in a list-making mood because I also have made a list of those things for which I am very thankful during my stay, and also a list of what I have learned being here—about myself, this place, and in general.

Things I am thankful for:
— No major illnesses (malaria, hepatitis, etc.)
— No major injuries (shoulder acting up, breaks, mobylette fall)
— No thefts (wallet, camera, mobylette)
— No enemies to make life uncomfortable
— No major job problems (dissatisfaction with my work, money problems)
— Not sent home early
— Great deal of autonomy in my job and life

What I have learned living in Togo:
1. Patience
2. My habits
3. My spoilings
4. My lack of prejudice toward Blacks
5. To be less squeamish about insects, somewhat
6. What it will be like without structured classes for an extended period of time
7. How important friends are
8. How much I love my family
9. More French
10. Ewe
11. How to read a library book
12. How much I love to read
13. What I love to read
14. How much I need music

15. My coaching abilities
16. Basic care for a mobylette
17. What the Peace Corps is all about
18. Sewing
19. How strong my body is against bacteria, etc.
20. A business sense of responsibility and rights as an employee

Well, everything is absolutely ready for Paris. My replacement comes in August. Once he is here, I'll have a fun, easy-going, relaxed, high-paced 10 more days to just relax, see friends, read, play basketball and work out. It's a nice wind-down to my year here.

A tantôt.

Love,
Bruce

July 14, 1982

Dear Family,

The strains of this fantastic adventure in Togo seem to have winnowed out the weak relationships in my life and exercised the strong ones to an even more potent level. Not only have we communicated more this year than ever before through endless correspondence, but we have shared countless more strokes in many imaginative ways than in any other year. I have gotten to know more about you, and you about me, as we try to fill sheets of paper with thoughts. In the interest of not taking too much time, we try to make the thoughts significant or special, even if about the most mundane aspects of life.

As my final days in Togo come round on my calendar, I have been thinking about what has been the distinguishing element of the year. Last year, toward the end of my sophomore year, I realized and classified a distinctive aspect of each of my first two years at Harvard, away from home and in the "real world."

I called my freshman year the "Year of the Woman." I went from high school sweetheart Jeanne to an endless rainbow of females, dates, attitudes, thrills, traumas, and lessons. From platonic to passionate. Top of the Hub to Elsie's Kitchen. Peach brandy floats to Bailey's chocolate malted frappes. The entire year was a lesson in women's sexuality, thoughts, feelings, attitudes, and manners. I treated and was treated. I made passes and received passes. I shunned and was shunned. It was fascinating and exciting, and most of all, an invaluable epoch in my maturity.

My sophomore year became quite symmetrically the "Year of the Man." Whereas my freshman year roommates gave me as many perspectives on women as on men, my sophomore year roommate, Steve, became an intimate companion unlike any I had ever had. Freshman year, my roommates discussed women per se. Steve and I discussed women and how they affected the other roommate. Freshman year, women were constantly putting me to the test and giving me incentive to be my best. Last year, the demanding personality of Steve challenged me to be my best in entirely different areas. Instead of dressing up my best, I rowed my best.

It was consummately appropriate that Steve and I go through the ordeal of joining the penultimate male institution and rite-de-passage of finals clubs virtually step by step and hand in hand. The finals club and Phoenix Club experience speaks for itself in its submersing me in the male culture of backgammon, cards, economic discussions, all-male lunches, fraternity.

Other aspects of life added to this dominant character of the year. The chummy attitude of living in Lowell House prompted more beer blasts with buddies than dinners with dates. Even our crew took on a more dominant aspect as I played that one sport for the entire year, staying with and getting to know very closely one team of guys more than I ever had before.

Which brings me now to Togo. It would be hollow to call this the "Year of Africa," as much as it would if I called freshman year the "Year of the Yard" and sophomore year the "Year of Mount Auburn Street." The setting is merely that which prompts a particular lifestyle or set of life lessons, but does not hold those lessons itself. I had anticipated that this would be the "Year of Myself." Being in Africa, really on my own in all respects, cut off from all relations and friends. But this has not turned out to be the case.

I would have to call my year in Togo the "Year of the Family." Contrary to being cut off, I seem to have become closer than ever to that hodgepodge in the pumpkin-colored house on Newbury Road. I've just realized the nature of this year recently, and I admit that it's quite early to come to such an analysis. I have not quite figured out all the dynamics of what made the year that was. It's sort of a combination of things, as always. This year's absence from you has made me realize the truth of something Dad said in one of his sermons, "You don't appreciate parents till you've left them." Not having gone far for school, this was the first time, really, that I left the family.

Obviously, this year's character has meant a great deal for my own maturity in this, my so-called Third Official Epoch. I now look to next year and try to anticipate what lies ahead. Will I ever have a "Year of Bruce?" Is that possible for my personality? Will I ever have a "Year of the Many," or is that my general, continual lifestyle? Or did these two designations take place alternately, or even simultaneously, during my young "Ipswich Years?" If the answers to the first two questions are no, are there any "Years" left? If not, that implies I have reached my goal of emotional and intellectual maturity with no major areas of life left to struggle through and discover. That seems unlikely.

Will there be a hiatus of development? A sort of vacation from maturing as I finish school and enjoy the fruits of my development? I'm sure sooner or later a "Year of the Spouse" and a "Year of the Child" await me. But are there others? Up to now my epochs have concerned relationship types, but can there be a concentrated experience and lesson to do with other matters? Religion? Job/career? Philosophy? What other relationships exist besides female-friends, male-friends, and family?

Lots of questions. Only answers await.

Love,
Bruce

Going Home

In the end…we will find that the boy we once held
in our arms has moved through the stages of
adolescence, beloved by us and protected in our
world, and has become the man we always dreamed
of nurturing. The best of adult life awaits him.

—*Michael Gurian*, A Fine Young Man

Toward the end of Bruce's adventure, he calculated that there were only 43 days until we would see one another for the first time in almost a year. When the time came, he flew to Paris via Abidjan. We flew via London to meet him.

The Brulé family that had hosted Sharyl during her two-week high school field trip to France invited us to stay with them while we were in Paris. After a happy reunion and enjoying the sights of Paris, Bruce, Ed, and I were to continue our vacation in Amsterdam and then in London. Sharyl remained at home with Grandma and Grandpa.

Within three days of our arrival in Paris, however, Bruce quickly became sicker and sicker. We conjured up all kinds of reasons for his illness and lack of appetite, from smog in the air compared to Africa's cleaner air to rich French foods. The doctor at the local clinic informed us that he had hepatitis. This diagnosis meant an immediate trip home for Bruce, while Ed and I, with our tickets already paid for, continued on with the rest of the scheduled trip. Grandma and Grandpa, along with Sharyl, took over the task of nursing Bruce back to health.

He recuperated. Ed and I saw Europe for the first time. And Sharyl got to hear many, many tales of Africa at her brother's bedside. A few months after we arrived home, Bruce returned to school and we packed away the mementos of our trip, along with the many letters Bruce had sent us throughout the year.

Twenty Years Later

EPILOGUE
by Bruce Lynn

After that year in Togo, my first step back into the Western world was a stopover visit to Europe, where I was to meet up with my parents. I had tried unsuccessfully to find a way for them to visit me in Togo, so we settled on a trip to Paris, Amsterdam, and London—their own bold adventure, as it was their first time abroad. Unfortunately, several days into the stay in Paris I became desperately ill. At first, we thought it must be either severe jet lag or shock to my system from all the rich food, but when I visited "le médecin," she inquired, "Didn't you notice that he has turned yellow?"

Viral hepatitis was very common in West Africa, and all of the other American students had contracted it at some point during the year. Still, months of dodging any serious ailment, gradually "going native," led me to grow increasingly lax about the food I ate, my general hygiene (for instance, how thoroughly everything was washed or disinfected), and medical safeguards. Most notably, I had let my gamma globulin inoculation expire, partly because there was some debate about its effectiveness. So even though my year away had brought me closer to my parents through our letters and other creative messages—telex, tapes, care packages, and a grand total of two three-minute phone calls—our one plan to spend time together, face to face, fell apart as I was loaded onto a plane for an early return home to recuperate while my parents completed the trip.

Togo remained a prominent part of my life through my last two years at Harvard. My history and economics major focused extensively on African history and development economics, where I could extend and apply the insights I had gained from firsthand experience. My senior honors thesis was an account of the entry of the Ford Motor Company into South Africa and the incentives and motivations that drove its investment there. (My year in Togo simply had not produced enough economics-oriented material for thorough treatment of a Togolese topic.) I returned to Togo twice

163

during my junior and senior years to assist with press trips organized by David Apter and Associates.

After graduating from Harvard, I went to work as a researcher for the management consulting firm Mercer, a fairly conventional first career step for Ivy League liberal arts majors. In addition, I started a side venture to import Togo's beer, Bière Benin, into the United States. As I mentioned in the letters, Bière Benin was one of the true delicacies of the country, a legacy of Togo's being one of the few colonies under German control until World War I, and of its relatively high-quality water system. Bière Benin was exported throughout West Africa. As specialty imports were hitting a peak of popularity among yuppies in the United States, I thought an African variant might have appeal.

Unfortunately, people associated Africa with negative images of disease and famine (Bob Geldof's Live Aid concert had just taken place). The typical launching point for ethnic beers was ethnic restaurants—but there weren't any sub-Saharan African restaurants. Our one initial order fell through when the distributor became overwhelmed by the demand for Corona beer. Soon after, the market for premium specialty imports fell sharply as domestic microbreweries took off. That was the end of my venturing into beer imports.

The cleanly demarcated annual rhythms of my life, described in my July 14 letter, seemed to fade away as I left the academic cycle. "Years of Whatever" did not materialize as crisply as I had expected during my student life. Broader, multiyear epochs became the norm.

The "Year of Meeting My Wife" materialized sooner than I had expected. A few months after graduation, I met Lori Isley at the local fitness center, where she was taking dance classes and I was keeping in shape. Lori was finishing her master's degree in vocal performance at Boston University. When I first saw her walk into the Center, I told the instructor that if she introduced me to Lori and we got married, I would give her one of my workout shirts (actually a Harvard rowing shirt that she coveted). She introduced us. Lori and I met for a workout together that weekend, I cooked dinner for her on Monday, she cooked dinner on Tuesday, and on

Wednesday I asked her to marry me. She accepted. The next week, we invited the instructor to my place for dinner. We presented her with the freshly cleaned and pressed rowing shirt as we announced the news of our engagement. We married six months later in North Carolina.

Our initial "Years of" were the "Honeymoon Years"—the prechild years of our marriage, when we focused on the new dimensions in our lives. We were building a relationship, a home, careers, and still, in retrospect, having opportunities for fun and spontaneity while living in the heart of the vibrant city of Boston. Then came the "Preschool Child Years," when freedom was replaced by the focus on two delightful children in their formative years. Finally, the "School Years," where we have been for the past decade, marked a major step of independence for the children and subsequently for us. Lori has been able to re-immerse herself in her career as a classical singer and other interests, and I have been able to resume pursuits such as sports — and reading books that don't have animals and magical creatures as the main protagonists.

Although settled down with a wonderful family (Isley is 15 and Chase 12), excitement and exploration remain very much a part of our lives. All of us began our own world adventure when an opportunity presented itself for me to relocate to England. I had always been fascinated by computers and took computer science courses for electives at Harvard, but never thought to look for work in that field because, compared to the concentrators in my classes, I felt I knew too little. However, when I joined Mercer in 1984, the personal computer (PC) was just coming into prominence. When my superiors there found that I knew how to turn one on, my work soon became dominated by computer programming and modeling. I found I knew more about computers that I had given myself credit for, and enjoyed the field more than I had expected. I subsequently took a variety of positions in software development and management until Kenan Systems presented me with the opportunity to set up a branch operation in London. After a few years, I took a position with Microsoft in the United Kingdom, where I am still employed.

The culture shock of our move to London caught me by surprise at first, which is not uncommon for expatriate Americans living in

England. Because so much of American life pervades the British culture — TV shows, movies, food, stores, restaurants — we were easily seduced into thinking that we had simply moved into a more cosmopolitan and quaint corner of our native country. We soon realized that the attitudes and perspectives are markedly different. Even the language is as much a difference as a commonality. As one adage describes it, the United States and the United Kingdom are "two countries separated by a common language." We had planned to stay in the UK for two years; ten years later, we are still here. I continue to love to travel: in the past year, I have visited Moscow, Egypt, South Africa, Mauritius, and Italy. Email and traditional holiday update letters have replaced written letters to share these experiences.

As in Africa, one of my favorite activities on these excursions is to pack my suitcase full of books I've been waiting to read. The arrival of the Internet has made reading material far more accessible, through rich on-line collections of material, and through simply finding and ordering the conventional paper works through on-line stores such as Amazon. I still play basketball in a local Wessex Division One league with the team Woodley Harriers. My coaching is limited to introducing various friends and family to the sport of sculling on the nearby Thames River, the mecca of rowing. We belong to the Marlow Rowing Club; its most notable member was Steve Redgrave, famous for winning five gold medals in five consecutive Olympic games. Friends come with me for one or two outings in a double scull, in which they can learn the basics of blade work and seat movement while I tutor them and help steady the boat. My most regular pupil is my son Chase, with whom I rowed in our first regatta in Swindon last summer. We came in third of four sculls in our heat.

With what, then, besides continuing some of the same activities, did the experience of living in Togo leave me? For starters, I have the loudest and most difficult keyboard technique imaginable, with some of the world's fastest three-finger typing. This legacy derives from the antique manual typewriter that I took to Togo and on which I drafted some of my letters home and every report and article I wrote for work. It seemed to require the force of a hammer to move the heavy mechanical keys. To make matters worse, I often had to make carbon-paper copies in triplicate. For any chance of making an impression on the back sheet, I had to use great strength to pound each key.

Writing is still very much a part of my life, though the electronic medium has supplanted handwritten and mechanically encumbered type. My reflections now tend more toward the needs and dynamics of customers and our staff at Microsoft than toward daily living and personal discovery. My most prominent letter writing comes with our annual holiday ritual of designing homemade Christmas cards (the two hundred origami Santa Clauses just about killed us) that incorporate the American tradition of an annual family update for far-flung and infrequently contacted friends.

My adventure in Africa taught me a great deal. While I had studied French all of my student life, I had never truly internalized the language until the year I was immersed in it living in Togo. I am conversationally comfortable in the language, which is handy in that we live just across the English Channel from France. I also learned much of the culture, history, geography, politics, and economics of a complex, different, and problematic part of the world. Those lessons are ingrained in me through firsthand experiences and vignettes that bring to life what I would usually absorb through reading.

While in Africa I experienced new extremes. I savored the luxurious extravagance of staying in a five-star hotel on travel-writer trips, and endured depths of impoverishment when money ran low and I had few alternatives for getting more. At times I was fitter than I had ever been, and at other times sicker than I had ever been. I experienced the most ecstatic days, and the most miserable. I had warm and rich family-like relationships, as well as periods of deep loneliness.

The greatest treasures collected from the year are the memories of experiences that were uniquely African. Safari. Locust swarms. The daily lunch of rice, peanut sauce, and goat intestine (sounds awful, but it was delicious in a "spécialité de Normandy" kind of way). Deep-fried yams with piment sauce. Bargaining with the market ladies.

The adventure was also filled with many dangers, indelibly imprinted in my memory by virtue of the adrenalin overdose they stimulated. Riding exposed on my little mobylette amid the chaotic Lomé traffic. Flying in an airplane bought from the Communist Polish airline when it was too run-down for them (they themselves bought it from Aeroflot when Aeroflot no longer considered it suitable, and Aeroflot had the worst safety record in the world). My seat belt was a rope tied around my waist and, yes, there were chickens running up and down the aisle. My one meager life-prolonging gesture was to decline the in-flight snack, which was some unidentified meat substance between two stale pieces of bread. I swam in shark-infested ocean with an undercurrent that tossed me around like a washing machine. On one occasion, when I was running late for a meeting, I foolhardily bolted into a presidential compound, the Togo equivalent of the White House, and was nearly shot by concerned guards. Africa is safer than most people think, but there are plenty of hazards for incautious twenty-somethings.

One significant regret for me is the absence of lifelong friendships. Perhaps the most enduring tie has been with an American named Cynthia Slater, who taught at the American International School where I coached the basketball team. She married a fellow teacher, an Englishman named Nick. Cynthia and I met up once when they were living in London, and we exchange holiday greetings every year. I became better acquainted with Ablode Lawson, who also taught at the AIS, when he came to Boston to study and eventually married there; however, we have since drifted out of contact.

My closest friend throughout the entire experience was André Akou. Western educated and active in the American community, he was a connection introduced to me by David Apter, and we bonded immediately. I don't know how I would have survived the year without his constant generosity and guidance. He seriously dated one of the American students and thought they would stay together, perhaps via his joining her in the United States. When she returned to California after an unceremonious separation, he became quite bitter. The experience overshadowed our own friendship until at the very end we became quite distanced.

The friends with whom I had the most open and honest relationships were my Aiglon basketball teammates. Apparently sports were the great leveler. We had a connection based on shared experience and mutual self-interest. It was these Togolese friends whom I most appreciated, especially in the Bar-Tabac after a training session, sipping our Bière Benin and sharing stories of our respective student lives and perspectives on the world.

My greatest regret is best described by the adage "You can't go home again." Two decades later, my African home of Togo is no longer the country I so loved. Not only is it different, as any place would naturally be despite the most nostalgic yearnings, but it has precipitously deteriorated. Since the end of the cold war, African countries are no longer vital pawns in the global geopolitical landscape, especially in the strategic chess matches played out in the United Nations.

Soon after the fall of the Berlin Wall, both Russia and the United States dramatically reduced their support for sub-Saharan Africa and its stable but expensive and dictatorial regimes. The result was a political vacuum that quickly filled with opportunists, revolutionaries, reformers, and profiteers in a chaotic mix of violence and revolt. Much of Africa experienced these new dangers, which led to the further flight of business and expatriates, along with their valuable capital and skills.

Although Togo has not been one of the prominent headliners of tumult and turmoil, it has suffered great upheaval. I recently spoke with a Peace Corps volunteer who returned from Togo a few years ago. She described a country that is a shadow of the hopeful little enclave I once knew. Delapidated buildings. Crumbling roads and infrastructure. Physical danger and violence. I had always dreamed of taking my wife and children to this wonderful country, whose art graces the walls of our house, whose stories pop up regularly in conversation, and whose vibrancy wrote a major chapter in my growing up. Sadly, because of the inherent risks and the pragmatic realization that what I would show my family would bear little resemblance to the country I once knew, I have not yet made a pilgrimage back to Togo.

It has been a joy to relive that life of twenty years ago through the letters my mother extricated from obscurity and from which she has created this book. For my part, I still think of my collected reflections as a travelogue, of greatest interest to a long-term adventure traveler, such as a Peace Corps volunteer. My mother saw the experience as a coming of age for my sense of self, my worldview, and my relationship with my family. In retrospect, it certainly was all of those things—and if the letters provide a glimpse into that personal journey, then I am pleased.

When people ask me to recall the happiest moment in my life, once I have eliminated the obvious landmarks such as wedding day and birth of children, what invariably comes to mind is one of my days in Togo. I had just picked up a telex from the Hôtel de la Paix telling me that one of my projects had been well received by Apter and Associates. As I hopped onto my mobylette and zipped down the ocean road toward the American International School to join a game of volleyball, the palm trees swayed in the ocean breeze, cooling the warm African afternoon. I felt that everything in my life was just perfect. And it was.

ABOUT THE EDITOR AND HER SON

Marjorie Lynn is a graduate of Goddard College with a degree in English. After leaving her job as a writer and editor at the MITRE Corporation, she devoted herself for 22 years to serving families, youth, and children as Executive Director of the YWCA of Newburyport, Massachusetts, a position from which she recently retired. She has been active in community organizations, including service on the board of Harbor Schools and Family Services. Marjorie lives in Ipswich, Massachusetts, with her husband, the Reverend Edwin Lynn. In addition to her son, Bruce, she has a daughter, Sharyl, and four grandchildren.

Bruce Lynn has worked in a variety of technology positions, developing and marketing computer financial models, artificial intelligence expert systems, multidimensional decision support systems, and Internet platforms. He joined the Microsoft Corporation in the United Kingdom, where he is currently Director of Network Service Providers. He lives in Marlow, England, with his wife, Lori, his daughter, Isley, and his son, Chase.

Printed in the United States
1079300003B/73-360